DATE DUE

BAM!

Bust A Myth

Delivering Customer Service in a Self-Service World

Barry J. Moltz

and

Mary Jane Grinstead

authorHOUSE®

AuthorHouse™
1663 Liberty Drive
Bloomington, IN 47403
www.authorhouse.com
Phone: 1-800-839-8640

First published by AuthorHouse   1/21/2010

ISBN: 978-1-4490-0794-2 (sc)

Printed in the United States of America
Bloomington, Indiana

This book is printed on acid-free paper.

Dedication

From Barry

To Biruta, because my wife, Sara, can't bear to read my books since she lives it.

To my sons, who are afraid of what I might say to the server every time we go out to dinner.

From Mary Jane

To Phil Grinstead, who is always there for me as a reader, supporter, and friend.

To Molly, Samantha, and Kyle, just because.

Acknowledgements

From Barry

Of the three books I have written, this was the easiest book for me to write. This book just flowed out of me since customer service has always been a passion of mine. My greatest joy in writing this book was to work closely again with **Mary Jane Grinstead.** She was my mentor twenty-eight years ago when I started IBM in Chicago two weeks after I graduated Brandeis University. One of the best parts of this book was melding what we believed about customer service into one coherent book. We could always build on each other's words. Mary Jane was the one that kept us on course.

Jun Shihan, Nancy Lanoue, and Kyoshi Sarah Ludden, my Seido Karate teachers at Thousand Waves, teach me the meaning of serving others by being a student and teacher. They have always given me encouragement to achieve the improbable. Deep bow and Osu!

Vered Arbel, who keeps the tightest boy in American moving, so he can then sit for hours.

My parents, **Alan and Carole,** who are probably the only people that read and spell-check everything I write.

Mike Cooper, my father-in-law, may he rest in peace, was an inspiring businessperson to me and always would find exactly what the customer wanted.

Shelly Malkin, at Perl Mortgage, who exemplifies what outstanding customer service is in every time I talk with her.

From Mary Jane

Barry Moltz, a friend, trusted partner in business, co-author, and an all-around whoosh of fresh air, who, when I was wrapped around my axle writing my first fiction book, suggested, "Why don't you try a little business writing…I think you would enjoy it." Ten years later, my free-lance practice is flourishing. Writing this book with him has been a delight. His passion for customer service in contagious, and his keen eye for customer service myths that need busting put his special brand of energy into this book.

June Cope, my mother, who at ninety-two is an inspiration of independence and a role model of graciousness, patience, and courtesy. Our family trip to Disneyland with her contributed to this book.

Rusty Cope, my father, who wasn't much on reading books (although if he were still alive, he might try and read mine), but always treated his customers as if they were friends—and they were.

Ray Cope, my brother, a highly successful entrepreneur who started his own company based on the highest levels of customer service to the surgeons, nurses, and hospitals he served. Even after selling his business and building the boat of his dreams, he continues to have a keen eye for both sides of the customer service equation—how to deliver *BAM!-good* customer service and how to be a *BAM!-good* customer.

From both

Katherine Stoica and Gal Arbel, who did basic research and interviews for this book. Without them, it would just be one long bad customer service rant.

Sophie Michals, who provided proofing and editing when we couldn't read another page or put in one more punctuation mark.

Paige Wheeler at Folio Literary Management, who continues to guide Barry along the path called publishing a book.

A huge thank-you to all the people who shared their stories on customer service. We laughed and lamented with you over your inspiring and depressing customer service stories. May we never have to experience some of the things that you have gone through. Ever.

A huge thank-you to those companies and individual employees who continue to provide *BAM!-good* customer service in this self-service world. You set the bar for us all.

And a not-so-huge but equally sincere thank-you also to those companies who contributed to this material by providing the opposite of *BAM!-good* customer service. May you benefit from our experience in the spirit it is intended.

Contents

Preface xiii

Introduction xv

Chapter 1: The Myth Busters 1

Chapter 2: Defining Customer Service
the Way a Customer Does 21

Chapter 3: Determining the Value of Customer Service 51

Chapter 4: Why Don't We Deliver the Customer Service
We Say We Want to Deliver? 73

Chapter 5: The *BAM!-good* Customer Manifesto 101

Chapter 6: How to Deliver *BAM!-good* Customer Service
in a Self-Service World 125

Chapter 7: For Customers Who Color Outside the Lines:
Delivering for the Best and Worst Customers 149

Chapter 8: Take Action: What Do I Do Now? 167

Appendix: Things You Want to Remember from This Book 179

Notes 203

Index... 207

Preface

Remember when selling stuff was as simple as opening a store in the local mall? Hanging a shingle and then adding up the sales? Sure there were always those brave souls who would venture to a store in the next town or to a catalogue to buy stuff, but most customers preferred to keep it simple.

Who knew that those were the good old days? Welcome to today where we can type a UPC code into our iPhones and get a price comparison for whatever product we're considering buying. Immediately. But it doesn't stop there. With just a few clicks you can be the proud owner of the new product at the Web's cheapest price.

Science fiction? Nope! It's a tool that's already in millions of your customers' pockets.

BAM! is an antidote to this turbulent new marketplace. It covers the myths of taking care of customers, including my favorite, "We need to under promise and over deliver." This book tells you why that isn't the case anymore. This book will also challenge you and your business to take a hard look at who you are and where you're going.

But it's not just a book about problems; it's chock full of solutions. Think of *BAM!* as the ultimate balm for whatever ails your business in sales or customer service.

I have a simple theory about business books. Most of them needlessly kill trees because they just repeat what's already been published countless times before. This is not just hyperbole; I get between four and seven business books sent to me each week by publishers. And most of them are just a waste of paper and ink.

That's why it's so great to be excited by a book. To feel that it has a fresh approach that can really help people in the trenches increase revenue.

Thought you've heard it all on customer service? Think again. *BAM!* walks you through the steps to creating your own strategy to help your company remain relevant and necessary by tailoring your product or service to your customers needs. Customer service? You bet.

Kudos to Barry and Mary Jane for taking a subject that I thought I knew a lot about and teaching me a thing or two. Or three. Or four. Okay, you get the point.

But don't just read this book. Do it. Now.

Bob Rosner
Syndicated columnist of "Workplace911" and author of *The Boss's Survival Guide*.

Introduction

Customer service has been turned upside down by the self-sufficiency and immediacy of shopping and buying products and services on the Web. Our self-help culture has been transformed into a self-service culture with customers able and willing to do much more for themselves. At the same time, we are becoming accustomed to the benefits and good feelings that we experience online through automated buying experiences that can be customized and personalized to our schedules, locations, tastes, buying patterns, and desires.

The Internet provides extensive alternatives and multiple sources for almost any product or service a person wants to buy. Add that to buyers' virtually unlimited ability to shop and price-compare online, and it is easy to see how customer loyalty could become more a thing of the past.

More than ever before, the transactional relationship between the seller of products and the buyer of those products is critical to companies' overall profitability. Except for economic monopolies, only companies that deliver excellent customer service make money.

In this increasingly transparent world where so many products and services are viewed by consumers as commodities, providing exceptional customer service becomes the only sustainable competitive advantage for creating customer loyalty. The harsh economic realities that every business faces today and for the foreseeable future make this even truer.

BAM! debunks the twenty common myths of customer service—from "The customer is always right" to "Customer service means the same thing to everyone" to "Companies achieve customer service by under-promising and over-delivering." Customer service myths run the customer policies of many companies without anyone even questioning them. Unfortunately, this ensures that customer service will only be a "bolt-on" and not a part of the DNA of that company. Inside the DNA of most companies is where customer service needs to be in order to retain profitability.

BAM! replaces myths with a tactical approach that shows companies how to make more money through attitudes and actions that will help their customers *feel satisfied* in good times or bad.

We are two businesspeople who have spent most of our lives selling products, services, and ideas. We have both worked for large corporations, which we then left to start our own sometimes-successful companies. We write about business extensively. We closely examine the cost of everything we do. After spending significant portions of our careers in high-technology-products business, we are both in the business of providing professional services.

Customer service is important in any business, but at the top of the list in professional services. In our companies, delivering *BAM!-good* customer service measurably increases revenue, reduces cost, and makes doing business much more enjoyable for us and for our customers.

Barry shares such a passion for serving his customers that he dreams about it—the kind of dreams where someone is chasing him and he wakes up right before they catch him, or he has a test at school and he arrives late. He has dreams where he is sitting in a restaurant and he can't get the food he ordered before he has to leave for another meeting. He wakes up in a cold sweat screaming and yelling. It makes him realize how important excellent customer service is in business and how rarely he receives it.

When you meet Barry, you can see him wearing a button that says: *Just give me good customer service and nobody gets hurt*. He hopes it will strike fear into every retail establishment and set the customer service expectations higher.

That button actually got us thinking about the adjectives used to describe customer service. We call the kind of customer service that we (and we are pretty sure everyone) wants *BAM!-good* customer service. In our book, we talk about what that means and how to deliver it. Then we started thinking about what to call "bad" customer service, and it hit us that there is no such thing. Companies treat customers badly all the time, but this isn't customer service by any degree. It is bad, sometimes even abusive treatment and we ought to call it that. Let's stop sugarcoating it.

Bad treatment so permeates American business that many of us don't realize how little customer service there actually is until we go into the rare place that treats its customers like kings. Why do we as consumers put up with bad customer service? Assuming there is a choice to get the product or service somewhere else, are we too lazy to make a change? Is the barrier to exit too high? Or have we been lulled into expecting and accepting less and lowered our standards accordingly?

We always tell businesses that what is critical for their growth is a sustainable competitive advantage. Unless it is an economic monopoly, every business needs something that will keep customers coming back when someone smarter with deeper pockets comes into their business space and tries to squish them like a bug. We can't rely on patents or other such legal maneuvers. No, we need to rely on customer service for our customers to stick with us and keep coming back. It's really the best arrow in our quiver.

Most of us get so caught up in landing new business that we forget about the customers we already have. Our existing customers leave out the back door while we bring new ones in through the front door. Overall, the company loses in this revolving-door strategy. Unfortunately, most customers suffer in silence and too often businesses never know that customers are dissatisfied until they leave. By this time, it is too late.

Why another book about customer service? First, we like customers. We like them a lot. In fact, you could say that we love customers. We want them to succeed, and we want our services to contribute to that success. Second, we are in business to make money. It is impossible to give *BAM!-good* customer service without your business ultimately making money.

This is not another book just about customer service platitudes, such as "The customer should come first" and "The customer is always right." This isn't a book about great customer service stories or even horror stories. There are already too many of those stories out there. This is a book about businesses doing the right things to make money in a world that seems to be increasingly about self-service.

The move to self-service started many years ago with gas stations trying to save money (and lower prices) by having customers pump their own gas. It now extends to checking in at airports and checking out at grocery stores. Internet shopping has taught us to be extremely self-reliant consumers.

But a big part of the reason we are self-sufficient is that Web sites (at least the really good ones) are designed to make it easy and intuitive for us to shop for ourselves and by ourselves. Consumers aren't looking for handholding; they are looking for ease and efficiency.

Mary Jane recently went through a TSA checkpoint at O'Hare airport. When she commented to the TSA officer that the bins were in the wrong place and thus holding up the line, the TSA officer responded, "We just do the screenings; if you want to get through the checkpoint, you have to HUSTLE yourself." She was stunned and went to the plane thinking that interacting with machines (the Internet, kiosks, gas pumps) really is often preferable to interacting with many people who represent companies.

Why *BAM!*? There are plenty of myths and platitudes about customer service that every business gets caught up in with posters around their offices. "Take care of the customer and they'll take care of you." "Good customer service is free." "Good customer service is common sense." We don't subscribe to these. Our customers aren't always right. If common sense produced good customer service, we would see more of it, and good customer service is never free. But it can be worth every dollar a company spends—if the company spends it right.

We are a practical pair, and this book expresses our combined experience with our own companies and in the companies we have worked for and with. It is about attitudes and actions that produce a level of customer service that will keep your customers coming back and cause them to tell your friends that your business is a good one to do business with.

Most companies say they *want* to deliver good customer service, but too many companies *don't* deliver the quality of customer service they say they want to deliver and that their customers want and expect. In *BAM!*, we talk about those things that prevent companies from carrying this out—people, systems, and attitudes.

We will help companies and customers see that good customer service is a two-way relationship. We present a dollars-and-cents case for why caring about customer service is essential for both companies and their customers, and we help readers understand how company and customer expectations get so confused and mismatched.

This book helps readers figure out what they really believe about customer service. It offers ways to understand what the customer wants and needs. It teaches business owners and employees how to line up their beliefs with what their customers want, and provides specific actions they can take to deliver what their companies need.

We will recommend a customer service manifesto—a two-way agreement between companies and their customers. We will identify the barriers to both delivering *and* receiving good customer service and offer a tactical approach for both companies and consumers.

Remember: Everyone is somebody's customer.

Chapter 1:
The Myth Busters

Let's face it: customer service is confusing. Customers want it. Companies know they are supposed to deliver it. Yet sometimes it's like trying to put the feathers back on birds.

We hear the words "good customer service" so often, but what exactly is good customer service anyway? We tell ourselves we know it when we see it, but do we really?

Good customer service or no customer service, we all have stories that we love to tell, but as consumers, what are our expectations *really* of customer service? Is there a level of service that would satisfy us, or does the bar shift continually up and down? And if it does, what causes these shifts? As companies, what are the obstacles to providing the type of service we say we want to provide our customers?

It would be convenient for a company if doing "our best" on any given day was good enough to produce positive customer service experiences. But it isn't, and trying to force it doesn't work. "Our best" isn't one thing or one set of things. Customer service is so confusing because it is trying to achieve consistency where consistency is difficult and maybe impossible.

As consumers and company employees, we aren't robots. We are human beings who change daily. While there are plenty of aspects to customer service that benefit from standardization and consistency— from Web sites to order-entry tools, customer service always boils down to the exchanges and relationships between people—and (luckily) people are still consistently variable. This makes customer service a moving target, difficult to figure out and even harder to provide.

Customer service is like current events. It's always relevant, and no matter how much you think you know about it, there is always something more to discover. In today's highly competitive, increasingly automated, technologically advanced, and über-price-conscious, self-service world, customer service is relevant for two reasons: First, customers and companies still care about customer service, and they care a lot; second, customer service is hard to do.

When we started this book, there were **81,728** titles on Amazon.com about customer service. That says that there is plenty of interest and no one way of doing it right.

Bust A Myth!

Customer service has the fascinating quality in every business to be simultaneously ubiquitous and absent. There probably isn't a company in business today—even economic monopolies behind closed doors—that would have the courage (or questionable judgment) to admit that poor customer service is part of its vision. Yet, we all know

2

companies that appear to deliver poor service so systematically that it almost looks like part of a plan.

On any given day, as customers, we experience countless examples of seemingly small and no-cost things that companies and their employees could do, but don't, to make our experience better. It seems so obvious that making the customer happy should be a natural, or at least a required, part of any business.

On the other side of the equation, as well-intended employees of companies, each of us can likely all think of plenty of experiences with customers who seem to be determined to remain dissatisfied no matter what we do. Some customers are demanding—and, yes, some customers are demanding beyond what is reasonable. There is even a reported case of a consumer suing a company because they were on hold too long!

However, when you think about it, it is pretty unlikely that there are many people who get up in the morning, put their feet on the floor, and set out to be as difficult a customer as they can possibly be. Similarly there are likely few employees who wake up planning to make customers' lives miserable.

So what is it that makes customer service so darn hard? Like any aspect of life that is hard to understand and explain, one reason customer service is so confusing is because so many myths have grown up around it.

Myths shape our beliefs and attitudes, but the thing about myths is that although they might have begun as stories to express a truth, over time the truth can be lost, and all that remains is a legend based on fiction that gets accepted and touted as fact. When, as companies and consumers, we accept myths as fact and base our attitudes and expectations on them, trouble follows. Even worse, we start to believe these myths so strongly that we post motivational signs around our offices encouraging our employees to follow these myths and telling our customers to believe them as fact. This can lead to dissatisfaction on both sides.

If we are to move forward into a new way of achieving customer service, we have some serious myth busting to do. Let's begin.

Myth #1: "The customer" is a single thing or entity.

The Belief: The reasoning goes that once I figure out the profile of my "typical" customer, I will be able to come up with a system to keep every customer happy and satisfied. Then all I have to do is give my employees this blueprint. As long as they follow it, they will satisfy "the customer" and the business will prosper.

The Reality: There is no such thing as "the customer" or even a "typical" customer. Different customers react to the same situation and the same service differently. The same customer can react to the same action and attitude on a different day differently from the way he or she reacted the day before. This is why satisfying the customer is so hard and many times out of reach. Self-service kiosks are the perfect example. Some people love them (road warriors in airports). Some people hate them (Mary Jane when she is checking out at our neighborhood grocery store).

And great Internet retailers and marketing companies set the tone for even more customer uniqueness by providing experiences based on our individual preferences, buying history, tastes, schedule, or geography, just to name a few.

Andy Alexander, *The Washington Post* ombudsman, states that "on a daily basis, a newspaper is going to disappoint (and often anger) customers because of its content. In my role as ombudsman, I hear from hundreds of readers each week who think *The Post* is biased in its news coverage—either too conservative or too liberal. Readers often are angry with opinions expressed on the editorial page that do not reflect their own thinking."[1]

Myth #2: The customer is always right.

The Belief: We should "act" as if the customer is always right in order to keep them happy when they are satisfied or to placate them when something goes wrong. Companies that profess this myth believe that *every* customer is too valuable to lose or that the risk of the bad press that may come from dissatisfied customers is too great for the company to bear.

The Reality: Let's face it, how could "the customer" always be right? First of all, as we have already said, there is no such entity as "the customer." There is only "this" customer. Second, no person is always right. There are going to be people who buy things from your company who are not right intentionally, or unintentionally. In fact, we'd be willing to bet that each of you reading this book can think of a time when you—as a customer—were dead wrong, but insisted you were right. Right?

Every start-up business opens its doors with the rallying cry that "the customer is always right" until they realize that it is economically impossible to build a viable, profitable business on the customers always being right.

In 1908, César Ritz, the celebrated French hotelier, was credited with saying "Le client n'a jamais tort," which translates into "the customer is never wrong." Many believe that "the customer is always right" is an American phrase that originates from this point, although it was not intended to be taken literally. There is a famous urban legend about a customer taking tires back to Nordstrom to return them (no, Nordstrom does not sell tires) and the sales people accepted the return. (This is puzzling because in today's automated systems, if the product was never in inventory, how could the sales person process such a return? Well, it is an urban legend, after all.)

Deborah House, CEO of The Adare Group told us, "Over my career, I've worked at McDonald's. I've had stores tell me of examples of when someone comes in and they don't want a hamburger, they want a grilled cheese, and they make them a grilled cheese."

Myth #3: The customer is always wrong.

The Belief: As business owners and employees, we know more about our business than the customer could possibly know, so when they disagree with us or offer a different point of view, they must be wrong. Customers are always trying to get something for nothing. Customers don't know what they want, so they should listen to us. We know what they need, and if they have a problem with something we have done, they need to give us a chance to explain. Once we do, they should listen to reason…our reasons.

The Reality: Customers are human beings. They will be both right and wrong. No company or business owner can have this much disregard for customers and remain in business. The only exception to this may be regulated or natural economic monopolies, credit card companies, banks, and utilities that treat you like a felon if you ask for customer service.

However, many companies do change their customer service policies based on customer feedback. Southwest Airlines changed their seat assignment policy because they received complaints. After receiving complaints from customers, Apple changed the Digital Rights Management (DRM) protection on some of its music to allow copying. Many companies used to have severe limitations on expiration dates on gift cards until their customers cried foul. Others haven't yet heard the cry.

Myth #4: Customer service is about having high-quality products.

The Belief: When a company has good products, customer service doesn't matter so much. It's the product that the customers care about after all. Good products don't need to be concerned about customer service since they will delight. As a company, if we invest in providing the products that best fit our customers' needs, they will be so satisfied that we won't ever have to deal with dissatisfaction.

The Reality: If only this were true. The best products in the world also have great customer service associated with them. Even good products break down and need to be serviced or returned. Even companies that produce great products need to anticipate competition and build brand loyalty. Eventually *someone* will make a mousetrap that is better than yours is and will have more money to promote it.

In the end, quality customer service will always trump the product and be the long-term sustainable competitive advantage. Apple's iPod is an example of a great product that works magnificently out of the box. Unfortunately, things go wrong with any mass-produced product. Just ask iPod owners about what they need to do if their rechargeable battery wears out. They have to send it back to Apple to replace it at a significant cost. This inconvenient customer service policy caused uproar in the industry a year after the iPod was released.

Myth #5: Customer service is just plain common sense.

The Belief: Good customer service is something everyone understands—like wearing a coat when it's cold outside or not touching a hot stove. All our employees have to do is stop and think logically about what the best thing is to do and they will be able to give good customer service. What we need is well-intended, rational people as our front-line interface to the customer, and we will be all set.

The Reality: How a person serving customers feels on a given day is influenced by a lot more than intention, intuition, or common sense. There are a lot of legitimate and appropriate answers to the question, "What would it take to give this customer good customer service?" My idea of "the best thing to do" may be very different from your idea of "the best thing to do." We could both be right, both be wrong, or sometimes be a mix of the two. That's why great customer service takes training. The basic attitudes and techniques of good customer service must be taught and learned by everyone, no matter how much common sense they have or how well-intended they are. Customer service is an acquired skill.

Zappos sends its new employees through a four-week training program so they can provide the best possible customer service experience. If good customer service were just plain common sense, this would be a waste of time.

Myth #6: The term "good customer service" means the same thing to everyone.

The Belief: As the company providing the product, attracting and serving the customers, and wanting to do our best, we have the data and experience to "know" what good customer service is—and because we know so much, our definition must be right. Therefore, since our definition of good customer service is the correct one, and customers do want good customer service, they must want what we are describing when we say "good" customer service.

The Reality: There are as many different meanings to good customer service as there are customers buying and employees delivering the service we are talking about. Why else could there possibly be tens of thousands of books on customer service on Amazon if we all shared a common understanding of what good customer service is? The customer service rep may think he provided good customer service but I, as the customer, may think he did not. A company may set a goal to answer all their phone calls with a wait time of fifteen seconds or less. I as the customer may get impatient at five seconds and pronounce it bad service.

Myth #7: Ethics, pride, and altruism are all reasons for providing customer service.

The Belief: Companies should provide excellent customer service because it is the ethical, honest, right thing to do. We should give good service out of pride in our company and ourselves. The people that the company hires should and do feel the same way. Psyching them up with this belief is enough to make them want to provide excellent customer service no matter what.

The Reality: All of these feelings may contribute to an individual's desire to provide excellent customer service when a company is doing well. For some individuals, these feelings may even be enough when the company is going through rough times. These standards inevitably fall when the company does not have enough cash flow to support the high standards. Customer service for some companies also suffers during difficult economic times as they start to cut services to survive. But in reality, for any company, neither ethics, pride, nor altruism is a sustainable motivation, especially when the company faces difficult economic times. The only sustainable motivation for providing excellent service is that will make the company more profitable.

Myth #8: If you learn how to "put up with your customers," business will be great!

The Belief: Customers are an interruption. We could be so much more efficient, do our jobs better, and provide them better service if they would just leave us alone. Why can't every interaction be self-service? One business owner even told us that if you are not careful, customers can put you "out of business!"

If they won't leave us alone on their own, we'll make it hard for them to get to us. That way, the ones who don't really need us will give up, and the ones who *really* need us will find a way to get through. By the time they get to us, they will be so grateful customer service won't be an issue.

The Reality: A profitable world that is free from the hassle of customers may be many business owners' secret dream. On our bad days, we have dreamed of this as well. The reality is that there would be no businesses if we didn't have the opportunity to deal with customers. Companies would be left in peace, but with a lot of inventory and debt. Many online retail Web sites when they first started out gave the customer no way to contact them by phone, to the great dismay of their customers. Thankfully, this is no longer the standard. Now, you can even find ways to call Amazon.com if you look hard enough.

Myth #9: Taking care of the customers you have is more important than getting new customers.

The Belief: It is easier to sell more to the customer you have than it is to go through the steps to attract a new customer. Also, it is more painful to attract and close a sale with a new customer than to keep the one you have happy enough to keep buying from you.

The Reality: There are a lot of statistics that seemingly support this kind of thinking. While it may be true that the marginal cost of selling an additional product or service to an existing customer is less than selling to a new customer (excluding a Bernie Madoff–like Ponzi scheme), it is also true that every business has some churn and will inevitably lose customers.

Existing customers leave because their needs change, they move, go out of business, or become dissatisfied. If a business is going to be sustainable long-term, it must both keep current customers *and* attract and close new prospects. This isn't an either/or proposition. Businesses need to attract new clients and retain the ones they have to be profitable and sustainable.

Myth #10: Unhappy customers tell their stories to more people than happy customers do.

The Belief: Unhappy customers dwell on their dissatisfaction and will talk, talk, talk about their dissatisfaction with a service or product. The reason to try to solve their problem is to get them to stop poisoning the reputation of your business.

The Reality: Stories about both good and bad customer service get around. People talk or, as Seth Godin says, people "sneeze." Happy ones and mad ones talk. Do the unhappy ones talk more? We don't know; there have been articles written that suggest this might be true.

In our businesses, we are not willing to take that risk. We need to find ways to get both types of customers to talk. Word-of-mouth references have the ability to spread more rapidly than ever before with the introduction of social networking. Web sites like Yelp!, Facebook, and Twitter provide a platform for users to exchange ideas and reviews about specific businesses. Social networking has become so popular that consumers, in terms of trust, are skewing their thoughts towards reviews posted by everyday people like themselves.

Myth #11: Unhappy customers are a part of doing business. If you handle a customer complaint well, the offended customer will turn around and be an even more loyal customer.

The Belief: There are multiple beliefs that support this myth. No matter what you do, customers are going to be unhappy; customers are going to complain. If you don't have any unhappy customers, then you are spending more than you have to on customer service. Just because a customer complains doesn't mean they are unhappy enough to stop doing business with you. In fact, it is almost okay for a customer to complain. Customer complaints are a way of getting customer feedback without paying for an expensive survey or a secret shopper. Plan on having some, deal with them the right way, and you'll have a customer who is more loyal than any happy customer would ever be.

The Reality: It may be true (sometimes) that when dissatisfied customers actually do come forward to complain (many don't) and you are able to resolve the complaint to their complete satisfaction, they will tell other people.

However, many customers are non-confrontational, and complaining just is not worth it to them. They just don't come back. Hundreds of complaints never make it to the company. People grumble in silence or to their friends. Or they get stuck or dismissed by low-level customer service agents. Then they stop doing business with you.

Barry tells about a recent experience.

"I booked a ticket with an airline but did not receive a seat confirmation. Upon arrival at the check-in desk, I was told the flight is full. Automatically I began to get worried and upset. I was a long-standing member in the airline's loyalty program, so the gate agent gave me an open seat in first class. The flight then became a pleasant and memorable experience that I told my friends about. But does it make me more loyal to the company? Not really, because this (not having a seat with a booked reservation) has happened to me before over the years—so guess what? I never entirely trust the airline, even when they give me a boarding pass with a confirmed seat. As a customer, I would rather know with 100 percent certainty that when the airline commits a seat to me, I have a seat, rather than knowing that on occasion, if there happens to be an empty seat in first class when I lose a seat that I thought was confirmed, the gate agent may bump me up to first class. For me, that bump really does not erase the sting."

Myth #12: Customers don't care about great service; they just want the lowest price possible.

The Belief: At the end of the day, the only thing a customer cares about is price. This is especially true during difficult economic times. Customers "know" that sometimes you have to cut service to provide a low price. They expect a company to compromise on customer service. If the price is good enough, they won't expect much customer service anyway, so why would a company spend money on that?

The Reality: If the product is a commodity and can be bought or received anywhere, customers may consider only the price. However, increasingly customers demand both low price and great service. Southwest Airlines started out offering low prices and giving service that customers thought was fine. Now they profess to offer low prices *and* great service. eBay started out attracting buyers with the lowest price. Now customers routinely look to buy from sellers with the best prices *and* the best reputations. We would much rather buy a product from Amazon new than buy it used from one of their resellers because we believe we will get better service.

Myth #13: Customers can't expect a company to fix all complaints overnight.

The Belief: Customers need to learn to have a little patience when something goes wrong. Every company gets overwhelmed at some time or other and people have to wait. Customers should understand that no business, no matter how well intended, can staff for every situation. Customers wouldn't want to pay for that for sure. Customers know that our company is well intended. They should realize that if they will just give us time to do our jobs, their problems will be taken care of eventually.

The Reality: This is a fast-moving, instant-gratification world where so many things are open twenty-four hours, seven days a week. Most people hate to wait. Unhappy people hate to wait the most. Waiting means something bad for your business—always. Having said that, waiting is inevitable—sometimes some customers are going to have to wait. An acceptable timeframe to your customers depends on what type of business you have. If they are stuck on a highway, waiting for a tow, their timeframe is probably accelerated. How many times have you received an e-mail from a customer service department saying they would get back to you in three days...three days in the world of 24/7? How did this make you feel? Satisfied? Happy? We bet not.

Myth #14: Forget about customer service; people buy from those they like.

The Belief: If your customers like you, they will buy from you. If they don't like you, they won't. Customer service from the rest of the business is secondary.

The Reality: For sure, building a relationship with a prospect or client is part of providing customer service. For many people, if you show you care about them, they will like you, and they will want to buy from you. In businesses with a lot of customers or prospects, it is not possible to get to know each and every customer.

If they like you and you are the person who will be taking care of them for the rest of their relationship with your business, this might be fine. However, usually it is someone other than the salesperson who takes care of the customer after the sale, so the customer has to like them, too. Many people follow service professionals from company to company. When financial advisors or CPAs move to another bank or accounting firm, many times they bring their business with them. When Mary Jane's attorney left one firm to start his own, she—and many of the other clients he served—went with him. When her hairdresser moved, she moved with her, but didn't stay long because she didn't like the policies of the new salon. Many people are inclined to buy from local small businesses only if the prices are competitive *and* the service is good. Just ask the business owners who have been put out of business once big-box retailers like Wal-Mart come to town.

Myth #15: Some people are naturally good at customer service.

The Belief: Good customer service people are like natural athletes. If a company can just find and hire them, then customer service issues will all be solved. People who love their jobs are the key to good customer service.

The Reality: Business is all about execution, and people are the key. But it is unlikely that a company will find very many great people who are as committed and dedicated to the business (and therefore to serving the customers) as the owners are. It is even harder to find them for minimum wage which is what a lot of first-line customer service jobs pay.

Myth #16: Comment cards and customer surveys accurately measure customer service.

The Belief: When asked, customers will be honest and tell a company what they think, whether it is good or bad. All a company has to do is ask the right questions, tabulate, sort, and analyze the answers, and we will know objectively how we are doing and what we need to improve our service.

The Reality: Voluntary surveys are skewed because the passionate people fill them out—as in the very satisfied and the very dissatisfied. The company gets customers at both ends of the satisfaction scale, and fewer in the middle, where most of the customers are. Also, people lie in surveys all the time.

Many times, companies do not get any actionable data from comment cards. They get a chance to solve individual problems or celebrate individual accolades for specific clients or employees. In order to see how you are really doing, companies must have a more systematic way to measure customer service. It needs to be ingrained in the process at many stages, not bolted on. Most restaurants or hotels solicit comments from their buyers immediately after the transaction. Some companies, like PETCO, offer $2 off or entry into a sweepstakes if you fill out their comment cards. Is this a bribe?

It certainly does not solicit unbiased feedback. Jewel grocery store employees have worn ribbons that say "Strive for 5" in order to remind them and their customers to give them the highest rating on the customer surveys.

Myth #17: Customer service systems should focus on troubleshooting. If it isn't broken, don't fix it.

The Belief: Good customer service is satisfying a current customer complaint. If the customer is really upset, they will say something about it. Then the company can be the "hero" by doing a diving catch. Customer service systems should be set up to be reactive, to handle customer issues, concerns, and complaints. Otherwise, a company is best served to let sleeping dogs lie. It costs too much to keep all the customers happy—and you can't do it anyway. These beliefs are companion to the beliefs that support Myth #5.

The Reality: Great customer service is anticipating when a customer will be unhappy and satisfying them before they complain. Why? Because dissatisfied customers don't always tell you they are unhappy, and unhappy customers can hurt your business in ways you know and in ways that you will never see. If you have dissatisfied customers, whether they complain or not, your business is doing something wrong. If you wait until you have complaints, they will be louder and more demanding. It only takes a handful of upset customers can bog down your entire customer service effort.

Myth # 18: Companies achieve customer service by under-promising and over-delivering.

The Belief: By setting the expectations of our customers low and delivering more than we promised, we will surprise and delight our customers.

The Reality: Customers are not stupid, and they live in a free-will zone. We do not decide for them what level of customer service is acceptable. They decide for themselves. What possible benefit could there be for a company that tells their customers they aren't going to do much—even if they exceed the low expectation that they set? This is a direct path to losing customers. We all get e-mails from companies after complaining that they will get back to us within seventy-two hours. They get back to us in twenty-four hours. This is not a good strategy. We are outraged at the seventy-two hours and then relieved at the twenty-four hours, but neither leads to creating a satisfied customer.

Myth # 19: You can satisfy all of the customers all of the time.

The Belief: There is a belief that if a company invests enough, trains enough, asks enough questions, listens enough, and really, really cares, then all customers can be satisfied all the time. There is also the belief that this is a good belief to try and get people to believe, even if you (and they) know that it can't possibly be true.

The Reality: Impossible! By pretending that this is true, a company can actually create more of a customer issue. Certainly this is demoralizing to employees.

Myth #20:. We left this last myth open so that you can supply a favorite myth of your own.

The Belief and the Reality: Our list is by no means conclusive What myth guides your view of customer service? What is your belief and what is the reality?

Attitude + Action

All of these myths get mixed in to the company strategy to produce, well, a mess. Instead of myths it takes attitude plus action to deliver customer service in a self-service world.

While it is impossible to anticipate and plan for every customer service situation, all companies can begin by following the principles of *attitude and action*. We define these as:

- **Attitude:** Make decisions with the deliberate intent of helping a prospect or customer feel more satisfied.

- **Action:** Take actions to create the perfect customer service experience from the customer point of view. Ask yourself, what would you want if you were your customer?

Marshall Makstein, president at eSlide, says that at his company, "Customer service is simple: a high degree of communication combined with an attitude of 'we'll do whatever it takes to deliver what you need (and more), when you need it.' We empower our clients to do their job better by delivering service and products beyond their expectations. We built the business and reputation by never saying 'no' to a client's request."

So how do you offer great customer service that lasts? Chapter 2 creates a new definition of customer service—based on the new belief that every customer is unique and that uniqueness creates unlimited permutations of the definition of good customer service.

Chapter 2:
Defining Customer Service the Way a Customer Does

Formulating a definition of good customer service for your company doesn't sound all that difficult, yet it's kind of like making a cat hold still while you give it a bath. Certainly there is no shortage of information on customer service available. We are drowning in surveys, studies, and reports that spell out customer service criteria by industry, type of company, or market segment. There are software tools and legions of experienced specialists and consultants ready to help well-intended businesses improve their customer service.

Some customers will tell companies in person, in focus groups, and in cancellation letters what they think good (and terrible) customer service is. Case studies of customer service are well documented, and for readers who prefer the real-time, anecdotal approach, all you have to do is raise the topic over coffee, as virtually everyone who has ever bought or sold anything will have an opinion and a story to tell.

So what happens with all this buzz?

Companies enthusiastically set up goals, policies, and measurement systems designed to deliver good customer service. They invest in training both large and small—and yet they still end up with unhappy customers. Why? Because the way businesses go about defining customer service is flawed. If a company is going to provide customer service that satisfies their customers, owners, managers, and associates have to accept that the definition of customer service is:

1. *Not* what companies say it is;
2. Almost never the same from customer to customer; and
3. A constantly changing, perpetually moving target.

Customer service is what the customers say it is

In each seller/buyer transaction, there are two independent points of view of customer service: the company's view and the customer's view.

The company's view is made up of all the actions a company takes to provide a level of satisfaction to customers and potential customers before, during, and after the sale. At a macro level, these can include providing a product or service that works as advertised; charging a price that customers are willing and able to pay; offering support for questions, training, installation, and use; ensuring on-time shipping or delivery, and defining a speedy process for problem resolution.

The customer view is determined by the level of satisfaction that an individual customer feels each time they use the product and each time they have an interaction with a representative—be it a person, Web site, machine, or automaton—of the company. Over time, which can range from less than an hour to many years, all these feelings accumulate to create one giant attitude toward the company.

Your customers could have only great experiences with a company for an extended time, and then bang! They can have such a bad experience that it will sour them from then on.

For years, Barry had a service mow his lawn all summer for $35 each time. Out of the blue, the last bill of the summer was $40. When Barry called to ask why it was higher, he received no response. When the next summer came around, he found a new service to mow his lawn. His former service lost the business essentially over $5 and an unreturned telephone call.

As important as a company's attitudes and actions are, customer service cannot be defined by what a company intends, does, or, for that matter, does not do. Instead, customer service is defined by *how satisfied or dissatisfied the company's customers feel during every moment of every interaction with the company and over time.* A company's relationships with its customer can be as tenuous as Barry's lawn service with him—and the scary thing is that customers know this, but companies usually don't.

Prospects and customers get to define whether the company's customer service is good or bad. That assessment is going to be calibrated by the customer's *feeling* of satisfaction. Much of the time this emotional computing goes on without customers or companies observing or even being conscious of it. When a company demonstrates an attitude or takes actions that contribute to making customers feel more satisfied, customers will feel, and hopefully say, that customer service is good. When a company takes actions that contribute to making customers feel less satisfied to dissatisfied, they will say that the way the company treats its customers is marginal to terrible—and they will say it frequently, loudly, and to seven people or more.

When companies define customer service by the attitudes they hold and the actions they take to serve the customer, they can spend a lot of money and still miss the boat if these attitudes and actions don't help a customer feel more satisfied. Companies that seek to provide a high level of customer service must consider how to positively affect the *feelings that lead to satisfaction* in their prospects and customers.

We propose a new definition:

BAM!-good *customer service* is *defined by the results of the attitudes and actions that a business takes to help a customer feel more satisfied.*

BAM!-good customer service is achieved when the customer *feels* satisfied. Every customer wants and has a right to expect this kind of service.

Definition of what customer service is not

Customer service is taking responsibility for satisfying every customer who is doing business with you. It is also means taking responsibility for satisfying the prospects who you think or hope could reasonably become customers. However, it does not mean compromising the company's integrity, morals, or self-respect to accommodate that rare customer that the company cannot satisfy, no matter what the company or any of its people do.

This is an important concept for a business to grasp. There are some customers that, no matter what you do or say or try, are never going to be satisfied. They will drag a business down. They will emotionally drain owners, managers, and employees. They will steal company time away from other more valuable customers.

Trying to make them happy isn't customer service. It is self-torture. Here are some indications that a customer is one of these:

1. Lack of respect or appreciation for the business owner's work
2. Excessive expectations or demands, either of the company or individual staff members
3. Unreasonable expectations in terms of monetary arrangements for work or goods provided
4. Proclivity for imposing difficult or unrealistic deadlines
5. Tendency to pay bills late, partially, or not at all
6. Treating the company as a commodity that can be discarded
7. Threatening to tell others, write letters, blast your company on the Internet, or skywrite

In fact, in July 2007, it was reported that Sprint Cellular showed "1,000 unhappy subscribers the door."[2] They sent letters to these customers saying that *"While we have worked to resolve your issues and questions to the best of our ability, the number of inquiries you have made to us during this time has led us to determine we are unable to meet your wireless needs."* Apparently, Sprint had identified about 1,000 customers of its 53 million who generated complaint calls at a rate of forty to fifty times higher than normal. According to Sprint, these customers would call from twenty-five to three hundred times a month, generating over forty thousand calls. We'll talk more about firing customers in Chapter 7.

Customer service means different things to different people

Attitudes and actions of customer service will be received and graded differently from customer to customer. This is inevitable. Why? Because every customer is unique. This is not something you probably want to hear. In business, we invest considerable time looking for the common thread among our customers so we can find leverage. We look for big problems to solve for big groups. We strive for economies of scale to hold down our costs and therefore our prices. We want to believe **Myth #1: "The customer" is a single thing or entity**.

We talk about "the customer" as if there exists one huge category of humans that, if not all the same, can at least be slotted into subgroups that have enough in common that we can treat them all the

same. In reality, each customer—no matter how many hundreds, thousands, or millions of them a company has—is a unique human being with feelings that can change from minute to minute, sort of like the crawler line across the bottom of the TV.

When you think about this reality for even a minute, it can become overwhelming. We would be the first to agree that no company can remain viable for very long by treating each customer uniquely (with the possible exception of those specialty businesses that serve the very, very wealthy). However, accepting that every customer is unique is the starting point for a company to develop a customer service strategy that helps customers feel about your business the way you want them to feel. The company owner and all employees have to believe that each customer is unique and have to hold the attitude that, if there were a way to do it efficiently and profitably, the company would choose to treat each and every customer as a unique individual.

When a new company is starting out and the founders are tightly engaged with a small number of customers, this isn't such an issue. Because relationships tend to be close and one-to-one, and a young company is flexible and still determining how they will treat their customers, it is easier to listen and hear the individual customer needs and to respond to them. In fact, there is a danger with young companies of too many one-offs.

Responding to those early customers often actually shapes how the company will respond to customers in the aggregate as the company grows. Russ Borrelli, a founder at eSlide in New York, told us, "When we started our company, it was easy to meet or improve on customers' expectations. When we only had a couple of clients, it wasn't as difficult as now, when we are spread a little thinner."

As companies grow, they have to find ways to be more efficient in all areas to stay profitable. It's natural and appropriate that they group their customers according to what they see as common. However, because each customer is different, one action on the part of a company can create very different feelings from customer to customer. In no area is this more likely than in customer service.

Problems in providing customer service begin when we start believing that if we just study our customers long enough, we can find enough common traits and desires to categorize them and treat them according to some aggregated set of feelings, needs, or desires.

Sometimes customers do categorize nicely, and there are enough potential customers with enough common desires that a company can create a product or service that fits them like a pair of spandex jeans. But eventually, companies learn that there are just too many categories to deal with, so businesses create product lines and service plans, often driven by price, to force customers into groups of the company's choosing, (friends-and-family calling plans, elite platinum flyers, self-service gas). The thought is that these groups of customers will match their expectations of customer service to the definitions the company sets out.

The challenge is that, while some customers do share common characteristics, expectations, and desires, each customer's feelings filter through what happened earlier and what he or she is planning to do next. This means that we must bust **Myth #6: The term "good customer service" means the same thing to everyone**.

In 2008, Lauren Freedman, president of the e-tailing group, surveyed one hundred retailers. In her results, she contrasted the reality of what retailers provide versus what the general expectations are. For delivery, the expectation was two days or next day; the reality was 4.76 days. The expectation for e-mail response was twenty-four hours; the reality was twenty hours and fifteen minutes. The live chat expectation was that people think it is required; the reality is that only 32 percent of those surveyed offered it.

Customer satisfaction is a moving target because customers' feelings constantly change

A rude remark, a crowded bus, a warm letter from an old friend, coffee spilled on a new rug, a 15 percent raise, a long line, a sick child—all can affect how a person feels while they are buying something from you. No company goal or customer service practice or policy is going to change this reality.

However, the opposite is also true. Customers give a lot of power to the people they buy from. A kind expression, a friendly word, a courteous action from a bus driver, a retail clerk, the receptionist at the doctor's office—all can change a customer's feelings about the day and your business.

Let's reframe customer service. Instead think about it as a chore, an obligation, or even a service we want to provide; consider customer service in terms of giving someone a better day. Instead of asking clients how is their day going—notice how that's often part of the script now when you call customer service lines—how about asking 'how can I make your day better'…not 'how can I serve you better,' but 'how can I make your day better?'

Just by asking this question, you have started with an attitude and an action that recognize how much depends on the feelings of the customer. If only there were words that could make people feel the way we want them to feel, we could be writing a book on the steps to take to make people feel good. Sure there are certain things you can do—be polite, be responsive—but there is no silver bullet, because so much depends on what else is going on with the customer on that day.

It would be great if everybody wore a mood ring. All we would have to do is look down at a person's hand, and if the ring stone were blue, we'd know that they were in a happy mood. Or if it were tan, we'd know that they were starting out from a less than positive place·

Moods and triggers—everyone has them. There is nothing harder than trying to anticipate the customer's feelings about anything, because feelings simply aren't rational. This means that a company can't possibly count on making all customers feel happy at the outset by meeting their unique needs and desires on any given day, because so many things that the company doesn't control go into making a customer feel satisfied. This means that the company has to figure out a way to deal with customers who feel unhappy.

One approach that companies have tried—without much success—is basing their customer service practices on **Myth #2: The customer is always right**.

 Telling employees and customers that your customer service practices are built on the premise that the customer is always right is like saying we all know the sky is blue, but we are all going to say that it is green. This customer-is-always-right approach doesn't promote an authentic commitment to customer service. Instead, it is a platitude with an adversarial setup for both sets of participants. If you want to trigger we-versus-they feelings between employees and customers, then go with this one.

If the customer is always right, then that must mean that in every situation where there is a different point of view (whether it is stated or unspoken), the company and its employees must always pretend to be wrong. Is that really a good way to have employees feel? Would you want the customers to feel that the company is wrong? Whether employees take it personally or not, this is a total setup. No customer is always right—but they are always the customer. The goal isn't to make someone right or wrong. The goal of *BAM!-good* customer service is to help the customer feel satisfied. Most of the business owners also agree that the customer can't always be right.

Susan Landa, owner of The Fossil Cartel in Portland, OR explains, "[My store] is in a mall, and mall policy is if the customer spends $25, you stamp their parking ticket for two hours, and sometimes they walk in and just expect us to stamp, but we pay for that, and sometimes we pay up to $6 for their parking. We also don't stamp certain lots outside the mall lot, because they're more expensive. If a customer spends $100 or $200, then we'll stamp it and tell them to please use the cheaper lot next time, but if they spend $25, and it costs $12 for parking, that's not worth it. And sometimes they get irate, and we explain to them that it costs us money. We have our boundaries too."

Manish Patel, CEO of Where 2 Get It, further warns business owners that "You have to first be careful so as not to take your company off course if you're building a product or a service, so there might be times when customers are unreasonable and you need to take appropriate action if they're too costly and not providing return. It goes back to relationships where you take money and provide nothing back, or alternatively you provide everything."

But Shelley Malkin, a loan officer, describes it as a two-way street: "At Perl Mortgage, we still believe the customer is always right. The customer is right in that 'this is what they want and how they want it done,' because that's their personal preference, but they may have factual things that are wrong, so it's your job to make sure they are correct in their knowledge."

While some companies try to make the customers feel satisfied by telling them they are right all the time, at the opposite extreme are companies that base customer service on the attitude that customers can't be trusted or don't know what they are talking about. These companies live by **Myth # 3: The customer is always wrong**.

The customer is not always wrong. This is the flip side of "the customer is always right"—with the roles reversed, making this even more adversarial.

Companies with this attitude only think a customer is "right" when what the customer thinks matches what the company thinks, because company owners and employees are confident that they know their business and know what "right" looks like. For example, let's say a customer ordered a pair of shoes and we shipped them an empty box. The customer and the company would agree that the company made a mistake; it's fairly black and white.

On the other hand, "wrong" can take on so many forms. The customer ordered a pair of shoes. The company shipped them on time, but the delivery person failed and the shoes arrived a day later than promised. Is that right? No…but just how wrong is it? If, as a company, we think that one day really doesn't matter even though we promised on-time delivery, this might not seem very wrong. The customer, especially if she is a high school senior who planned to wear the shoes to her prom, which happened to be the evening of the day the shoes were supposed to arrive, will be really upset. In this scenario, she (or her mother) is likely to have strong words for the customer service representative from the shoe company, who, in a customer-is-always-wrong culture, will likely wonder why, if the date was that important, the girl didn't order her shoes a few days ahead in case a shipping delay occurred. The answer, of course, is that the shoe store promised next-day delivery.

The reality is that customers are both right and wrong

An unhappy customer might be *right* that a policy that makes sense to your business doesn't make sense from the customer's point of view. The same customer might be wrong because she misunderstood or made a mistake. The reality is that customers are wrong all the time. Sometimes it's deliberate; more often it's a mistake. *Employees need to understand both sides of this truth.* Companies need to take into account how to train employees to respond when the customer is right *and* when they know that the customer is wrong.

Susan Landa at The Fossil Cartel explains her method: "I would say to be personable and gracious toward the customer. Seeing as close to eye-to-eye as possible, doing everything within reason for the customer, you have to be able to understand people in a way, because there are some people who will abuse the system for personal reasons, so you have to be careful how far you go, because it's not necessarily cost-effective or worth it. Every once in a while you get a customer who buys something and returns it, like she wants to wear a piece of jewelry for an evening."

Besides feelings, there are other things that cause customers' definition of customer service to change

The shifting bar of customer service makes it harder for companies to know what to do to meet expectations, and it also makes it more difficult for customers to know and express what really matters to them and how much.

Why? Have customers lowered or raised their expectations? Are things different than they used to be? Are customers responding to companies lowering or raising the bar on customer service? Or are companies responding to customers? Who is leading in this dance, and what *are* the things that cause customers' definition of customer service to change?

The competitors come out with a new product or service that raises the bar

In innovative industries, the competition is always coming up with something new. Customers are no longer willing to pay (because companies have to charge more) for a more service-oriented way of doing things: This is an example of a "contract" working for both. Done the right way, customers are okay with it and so are *companies*. For example, Zappos.com changed the rules in selling shoes to consumers.[3] Standard wisdom said that companies could not sell shoes by mail over the Internet because there was a high return rate (25 percent) when they were sold in stores. But Zappos proved this wrong by providing free shipping both to the customer and for returns from the customer. In this way, the Internet creates entirely new categories of products and services. It has changed the way products are ordered and delivered, and has redefined customer service—not only for mail-order businesses, but for companies that are bricks and mortar, too.

Zappos ships free to and from their Web site. As any college student who has ever worked in a retail shoe environment selling women's shoes knows, women like to try on shoes, lots and lots and lots of shoes. They also might be prone to start with a size that is smaller than the one they actually wear. How do you deal with this phenomenon if you are an online shoe retailer? Here's what Zappos does. All shipping is free. Period.

Last summer, Mary Jane ordered four different pairs of shoes for a wedding. They were all black silk and ranged from about $90 (she planned to spend around $100 to $150) to $350 (a pair of Kate Spades, which she included in the order just for fun, since Zappos's shipping both ways was free). Of course, she ordered the wrong size of the Kate Spade shoes.

She called Zappos, and they not only shipped a larger pair, they didn't even charge her credit card. "Just send back the ones you don't want," they said. Mary Jane had intended to buy one pair of shoes, $150 tops. She did, but she also bought the $350 pair of Kate Spades. Zappos maybe paid $20 negotiated shipping for all the back and forth, and Mary Jane bought almost $500 worth of shoes. She was delighted that she did—and the experience still felt wonderful when, after eight hours in her three-inch-high Kate Spades, she could barely hobble to the car.

Social and cultural attitudes and values change

We live in a culture of immediacy. We want what we want, and we want it now. This is even truer with younger consumers who grew up on the immediacy of access by the Internet. Things are also more egalitarian. Many people would rather do things for themselves than wait. Self-service gasoline pumps, ATMs, self-check-in for airplane trips, luggage carts at airports, and self-service soda fountains are some of the many examples of actions that used to be expected as part of good customer service.

However, if you want to understand the variability in customers' feelings about the quality of self-service, consider a study that we did for this book. The idea came about as we were discussing the acceptance of self-service. While we are a big fan of ATMs, generally positive about airport check-in kiosks, and mostly ambivalent about buying movie tickets from a kiosk, we detest self-checkout at grocery and big-box stores.

One of the grocery stores near where we live has self-checkout lanes for fifteen items or less. Every time we try to self-checkout, we have problems. Our frequent shopper card discount can't be read. The machine won't scan the broccoli. A voice tells us we need to "bag the item" when we have already put our dozen lemons in a bag.

As far as we are concerned, the only reason the grocery has those self-service lines is so they won't have to hire as many cashiers. Even though using one means we don't have to wait in a longer line, we leave the store feeling angry and frustrated, vowing never to return.

Mary Jane's husband, Phil, on the other hand, won't use anything *but* the self-checkout lanes. He doesn't see any problem with the equipment. If Phil needs to rescan his card or an item, he doesn't mind. He likes being able to arrange the vegetables in the bags the way he wants them to be, without the onions squashing the bread. When Phil concludes his transaction, he feels a sense of accomplishment and leaves the store feeling—you guessed it—very satisfied.

If the grocery store asked Barry and Mary Jane about their customer service, we would say it is terrible, while Phil would say that it is *BAM!-good*.

We surveyed 10,000 people to see what they thought of their self-service experiences when buying various retail goods and services.[4] Our survey told us the following:

Location	Usage	Good/Excellent
Airports	96%	83%
Movie Theaters	45%	84%
Hotels	24%	84%
Grocery Stores	70%	48%

Respondents' usage varied based on the type of service. The most commonly used applications were checking in at the airport and checking out at the grocery store. Self-service applications at hotels were still only used by 24 percent of the respondents. This may be because of the lack of lines at hotel reception desks or because there is something innately more important about being welcomed at a hotel. (Personally, neither Barry nor Mary Jane trusts a machine to give a good room!)

Satisfaction with using the applications did not vary, except for grocery stores. Like us, respondents were split on whether they liked the experience or not. This may be a result of how complicated the transaction is at a grocery store versus getting a boarding pass or movie tickets—or it may be that some people, like Mary Jane's husband, Phil, take to self-checkout and other people, like Mary Jane and Barry, never will. (We have included a list of respondent's comments in the Appendix.)

Just as there is no one-size-fits-all perfect customer experience, there is no magical set of actions that defines or will produce perfect customer service if you set out believing that the customer is always right or wrong.

Action + Attitude: Building a dependable link between your company and prospects and customers to produce the feelings you want your customers to have

We asked successful business owners (whose customers say they provide very good customer service) to tell us *actions* that demonstrate good customer service. This is what they told us:

1. Be personable and gracious toward the prospect or customer at all times.
2. Treat every person with dignity and respect.
3. Consider the other person's needs and point of view first.
4. Encourage customers to express their needs and desires.

5. Listen to what the customer needs and desires.

6. Provide customers with everything they expect, and then give them service beyond what they expect.

There are good examples that we found of each of these:

1. ***Be personable and gracious toward the prospect or customer at all times.*** When Barry was in Tokyo years ago, he went to the shopping district (Ginza) when the stores were just opening up. As he entered and walked through one store, the salespeople in each department bowed to him as he went by. Barry got such a feeling from that store that he just had to buy something. Fast forward to anytime you have waited for a store to open somewhere in America. They often don't open on time, and then, likely as not, someone will unlock the door begrudgingly, and without speaking, turn their back on whoever might be waiting. They are never ready for business when you enter—often sweeping the floors or straightening the merchandise, and if you interrupt these housekeeping tasks, you feel like they are doing you a favor by helping you.

2. ***Treat every person with dignity and respect.*** Accept that every person has a right to their own opinions and point of view, and that your treatment of them is not initially determined by their treatment of you. A prompt, friendly greeting acknowledging their presence, direct eye contact if you are one-to-one, and asking permission to put them on hold when you are connected via a phone line are all part of this.

   Scott Jordan at SCOTTEVEST tells us that you need to train your employees to simply treat customers precisely as they would expect to be treated in a similar situation. "No formal training manuals are provided," he says, "rather employees are empowered to handle each customer uniquely and provide incentives as needed to keep the customer happy. This does not mean that the customer is always right, because often they are not. For example, if a customer did not refer to the size chart before placing an order and expects us to pay for the return shipping for an exchange, the answer will be no, but if you deliver the answer in a respectful manner, the customer will understand. Now, if the customer ordered five other items over time and treats our employee with respect in asking for the exchange at no cost, then our employees are empowered to make an exception to this rule."

3. *Consider the other person's needs and point of view first.* People want to be treated with consideration—never more so than when they are thinking about spending their money or have already spent their money and have a problem with what they bought. One time when Barry was stuck on the ground for seven hours trying to get to Portland, he had to reroute his trip to get to his destination. As a frequent traveler, he did not complain to American Airlines. Barry flies thousands and thousands of miles every year, so he took it in stride. The next day, he received an e-mail from American apologizing for the trouble and adding 6,000 miles to his frequent flyer account. While 6,000 miles is really worth less than $100, the point was they were monitoring his travels and apologized *before* he could complain!

4. *Encourage customers to express their needs and desires.* Needs and desires may not necessarily be the same thing. "Customer service is serving the needs and desires of a person, and more

than serving the need is serving the desire," says Debbie Rosas, founder of The Nia Technique, a health and fitness firm. She compares a customer service person to being like an old-fashioned courtesan. "A customer may describe what their needs are, but my job is to also find out what they desire, so I will address the emotions of the individual. For example, they come to me and say' I need to lose weight.' If I just address their need to lose weight, I'm *telling* them they have to lose weight; they have to do this; they have to do that. Their desire might be to feel better more than to look better, or they might say I desire to have more energy. I then direct them to focus on the desire, which ultimately takes them to the need. Addressing the desire addresses the need. Their desire becomes the magnet, and that magnet allows them to hone their energy and use it in a very efficient way."

5. *Listen to what the customer needs and desires.* Shelley Malkin at Perl Mortgage tells us that "Good customer service is knowing what the client wants and answering the question before they ask it, and doing whatever it takes, especially in my business, to make the customer comfortable, because my business is one of the biggest transactions of their life."

6. *Provide customers with everything they expect, and then give them service beyond what they expect.* Sometimes *BAM!-good* customer service is a matter of inches. We both live in Chicago, and city buses here are a very big deal. More than 2,200 of them operate over more than 153 routes and 2,517 route miles. The buses are clean, heated, and air-conditioned. The Chicago Transit Authority (CTA) provides a terrific service that allows riders to use their PDAs to check on when the next bus is likely to arrive and if there are any unusual

delays. Fares have gone up, and people grumble about that, but basically the bus system works fairly well.

So when we head out the door to the bus, we feel neutral to positive about the experience. That can change in a heartbeat, depending first on the weather and then on the driver of the bus. If it's raining, for sure we are feeling less positive by the time we get to the stop, but when we see that the 76 bus is at the stoplight two blocks away, we feel a little happier.

As the 76 moves toward us, an absolute power shift occurs. It's unspoken and invisible, but without even thinking about it, we give the bus driver the power to determine how we will feel about the service we get from the CTA for the rest of the day.

The morning bus driver eases up as close as she can to the curb, which means that the tires of the bus don't splash the passengers, and it means that we can step from the sidewalk directly to the lowest step of the bus without having to wade through the water that pools at the curb. At that point, we are ready to do an impromptu commercial for the CTA.

We asked the same group of business owners to list the *attitudes* that demonstrate *BAM!-good* customer service—when demonstrating good customer service is defined as making a customer feel more satisfied.

1. Friendliness
2. Openness
3. Patience

Here's how those attitudes look in practice.

1. *Take care of the customer as you would want to be taken care of yourself.* The best way for a company to help customers feel satisfied is to think about how the people in the company like to be treated when they are buying something from someone else. Recently Barry entered the small grocery near his house where he shops, and the person behind the counter (whom he had never seen before) handed him the receipt and credit card back—with both hands—and said, "Thank you, Barry." This guy had Barry's credit card in his hand for all of twenty seconds, so Barry knows that he took a few extra seconds to read and use his name. It made Barry feel very welcome and as though his patronage was valued.

2. *See as close to eye-to-eye with the prospect or customer as possible.* Most people don't get up in the morning determined to figure out how to take advantage of someone else. Instead, most people get up and make the decisions they need to make to live their daily lives. These decisions include acquiring the goods and services from others that they can't supply to themselves. Whatever customers are buying, they are almost always trying to solve a problem.

   Mary Jane recently had a much different experience with American Airlines than Barry's rerouting example. She severely injured her foot, and was in a surgical boot with bandages and a cane. The day before she and her husband were flying on American Airlines to a family event, she received a letter from American Airlines with a courtesy one-visit pass for the American Airlines Admirals Club with a special offer for purchasing an annual membership at a reduced rate. (Like Barry, Mary Jane is a lifetime million-mile frequent flyer.) The timing couldn't have been more perfect. The logistics of getting to and through O'Hare airport with a damaged foot aren't easy, and waiting in the Admirals Club would be much more pleasant than sitting at the gate. She and her husband had been thinking about rejoining the club, so it would be a good test of what the Chicago club had to offer.

A wheelchair attendant took Mary Jane to the Admirals Club. She hobbled to the desk with her cane and showed the receptionist the courtesy card. The woman signed her in and asked if she needed assistance getting to the elevator. "No," Mary Jane said, "but would you direct my husband to meet me when he arrives? He was checking our bags because I couldn't stand." "This pass is only good for one person," the woman said. "He can't come in here." "It doesn't say that," Mary Jane said. (The pass said that it was good for one visit.) "Well, it is only for one person, and he can't come in. You can buy a membership if you want," the woman said. "I misunderstood," Mary Jane said. "As you can see, I have let the wheelchair go. I am a million-mile flyer of American Airlines. Could you make an exception for two hours and let my husband sit with me in the club?"

"Absolutely not," the woman said. "If I did that for you, I would have to do it for everyone who comes in here a free pass." "But isn't that why are offering the free passes?" Mary Jane asked. "So that people can come in and see what your clubs are like." Mary Jane ended up hobbling out of the club and waiting in the airport corridor for her husband to join her. In less than twenty-four hours, she went from feeling very appreciated and respected by American Airlines to being extremely dissatisfied and angry. Her experience at the Admirals Club was likely just the opposite of what the marketing person who thought up the courtesy card campaign intended.

3. *Apply the personal touch.* Barry stays at twenty-five to fifty different hotels every year. He usually arrives late and leaves early, and frankly, a clean pillow is a clean pillow, so they all seem basically the same to him. But a recent stay at an Omni Hotel stands out. Upon returning to the room to freshen up for his next round of meetings, he was greeted with a hand-written note from the housekeeper that said, "Good morning, Mr. Moltz. Thank you for staying with us! Have a safe trip home tomorrow. I hope you will come back soon. ☺" Wow. This made a huge difference in what Barry thought of the hotel, and helped differentiate Omni from other places he stays.

Ultimately the actions and attitudes that a company will take to produce good customer service will depend on the characteristics of the business, the industry, and the prospects and customers sought. Regardless, there are a set of actions that always, always, always apply. This list is a starting point for well-intended companies, regardless of how the transaction with the customer takes place.

We asked business owners to describe how they feel when they receive good customer service. "Satisfied," they said. "Okay," we said, "could you expand on that?" What else did they feel when they felt satisfied? Their answers: happy, full, confident, smart, relieved, secure, rested, appreciated, respected, and connected. For example, Carl Albrecht, president of PointManagement LLC, told us that "Good customer service is when the customer leaves every transaction feeling they came out better than even. I make sure at the end of every transaction we ask the customer how they feel in that regard."

How do companies and customers share the definition of *BAM!-good* customer service?

BAM!-good customer service is all about agreement and relationship. Agreement comes first, which makes setting customer expectations the most important aspect of good customer service, always remembering that *BAM!-good* customer service is defined by the attitudes and actions that a business takes to help a customer feel more satisfied.

The expectation of *BAM!-good* customer service becomes established in multiple ways.

1. **Deliberately** – from advertising, promotional, and educational literature; taglines; Web sites; and in-store displays
2. **Conversationally** – from associates trying to make a sale, presentations, and interviews
3. **Indirectly** – from individuals and organizations outside the business—industry association reports, watchdog agencies, and product reviews
4. **From what other customers say** – word of mouth to other potential and actual customers.

Too many companies think that they are defining good customer service when they tell their prospects and customers how good it's going to be instead of creating a two-way dialogue. (Sound familiar?) A more solid way is to replicate what eSlide does.

Russ Borrelli tells us that he bases everything on reputation. "We don't have a big sales force. The work that we get is because we provide what people want. When a client calls about a project, the salesperson assesses the request, prioritizes it along with their other jobs, and tells the customer what can be delivered in the time frame they need. Now we've branched out and started using statements of work for most of our jobs. It's a combination of a creative brief to clarify our understanding of what the customer told us, with the deliverables, the cost, and time frames. We started our business with people we kind of knew and had worked with before, so there was a level of trust, and we didn't really use statements of work. Then we worked with a hedge fund, and we sort of did one, but they were surprised at the invoice. There had been a lot of adjustments and a lot of tweaking to the job. Although we were paid fairly, after that we decided to lay it all out for every job."

Defining customer service the Disney way

What is the thing that many customers say they hate the most? Waiting in line. Yet, Walt Disney World in Orlando, FL, is entirely built around waiting in line. In fact, there are whole books written on line-management strategies for people planning to go.

Mary Jane's extended family recently took a family vacation to Orlando, doing the four Walt Disney parks in five days. She rode everything from the Tower of Terror (clinging to her goddaughter's hand) to It's a Small World (twice with her five-year-old niece).

Disney delivers on certain things, but the customer also has to be in the game. The lines for the most popular attractions can range from ten minutes or less when the park opens to more than ninety minutes in the afternoons when the parks are most crowded. There is absolutely no practical or affordable way for Disney to eliminate lines or waiting periods. For sure they aren't going to build a whole row of Thunder Mountain roller coasters so that there is an empty car waiting whenever someone wants to ride.

Instead, Disney has made line waiting an expected, acceptable, and even fun part of the customer experience. Moving around the park between the older and newer rides, the progress of Disney's learning in line management is evident. The earliest attractions are built right in the open. At the Dumbo or the Tea Cup rides, roped mazes of winding lines of waiting guests are right out in the open for all to see. As the line gets longer, a pleasant, smiling (more about this later) Disney employee adds more posts and ropes, making the maze longer and more circuitous, but there is no disguising the fact that you are waiting in line.

At the Haunted House, the feeling of the ride begins at the line, which queues along under a canopy that resembles the awning of a funeral home. Waiting riders walk past a graveyard with tombstones with humorous inscriptions. Some of them move—and you don't notice so much that the line doesn't.

A new twist that Disney has added is the trading of Disney pins. Visitors purchase a sash that hangs around the neck and a starter set of trading pins. Then they can trade pins with most Disney employees for free. The cool thing is that the employees have pins that aren't for sale and can only be gotten through trade. While the kids are waiting in line, they can trade pins with any Disney person who happens along.

But the real innovation that Disney has instituted in recent years is the Fast Pass. Here's how it works: A customer can insert her park pass and those of her party in a kiosk (there's that kiosk thing again) and get a ticket that will admit them to a "fast" lane for the most popular rides. The pass works for a one-hour window later in the day. What this means is that a group can get in line for one ride and designate a person to take everyone's park passes and dash to a Fast Pass kiosk to get timed tickets for another popular ride.

With the pin trading and the Fast Pass, Disney has turned line waiting into a game. Mary Jane's nine-year-old nephew felt a real sense of accomplishment when he scored the third trading pin in his Pirate's set, and his aunt felt relieved when she was able to secure a ticket on the *Rock 'n' Roller Coaster* that moved them ahead of a two-hour line.

Mary Jane calculated that the family waited in line at least four hours of every twelve-hour day. Were they satisfied with their Disney experience in spite of the lines? You bet.

The opportunity for *BAM!-good* customer service never ends

The opportunity for *BAM!-good* customer service begins the first moment a prospect comes in contact with a business, and continues indefinitely for as long as that prospect could become a customer or does become a customer who can continue to buy. This is why service departments in car retailers have become critical to bringing the customer back three, five, or ten years later to buy another car. The service part of the car business increasingly is also the more profitable one. Barry still has the Lexus he purchased many years ago, and keeps going back to the dealer for service. They not only lend him a car if he needs it, but if Barry decides to wait for them to fix his car, there are free drinks, Wi-Fi, and even a putting green!

The perfect customer experience

Is there such a thing as a perfect customer experience? If there is, can *BAM!-good* customer service bring it about? "A perfect experience for our customers would be that they pull into the car wash and their car is the first in line," says Jennifer Warden, co-owner with her husband, Eric, of Mustang Elite Car Wash in Grapevine, TX. Of course that doesn't always happen. But Mustang has created a lobby experience to make the wait better. There is a gift shop right in the waiting area for busy parents who always need some kind of card or a birthday present for a Saturday-morning birthday party. They sell cold drinks and there is a gentleman who provides superb shoe shines at a very competitive price.

"No matter how big the line is, it seems like by the time I browse through the shop—they are always getting in new things—then pick out my card and pay, my car is waiting outside for me, ready to go. I feel a real sense of accomplishment. My car is clean, plus I took care of two more things in just one stop," says one customer we interviewed.

Whether they can ever make it happen or not, every business owner can envision what that perfect experience would look like from the customer's point of view, and take the steps to try and make that experience real.

A business like Mustang Elite Car Wash and Lube Center must honestly care for and about its customers. Sure there might be one or two bad eggs, but for the most part, it pays to do business with people you like, and to like the people you do business with. For most successful business owners, caring about the customers is automatic. It often becomes less automatic the deeper you move into the organization.

How does a company build affection for its customers? First you have to like them. Maybe you are a person who naturally likes people, and so you are already inclined this way. That makes doing business easier. But not every person who operates a company or deals with people is a people person. That makes delivering customer service more difficult. They have to find reasons to like their customers. Revenue is one.

Your value is in your customer's minds; the value of your customer is on your financial statements

The customer may not remember the details of the transaction—what they said or what you did, but they will remember how they felt…and they will remember that feeling for a long, long time. You need to be able to convert this feeling into dollars and cents for your business to be profitable and grow. This is the subject of Chapter 3

.

Chapter 3:
Determining the Value of Customer Service

The idea that customer service is somehow an automatic requirement of all businesses gets drummed into us early and often. Should a company chase customer service because it is the "right" thing to do, like shoveling the snow off the sidewalk in front of the store? Is it a matter of pride or a matter of building a good reputation? Is there some kind of social, ethical, moral, or otherwise altruistic obligation to treat people right? Why do we say we want to deliver good customer service anyway?

Some companies are economic monopolies, like public utilities or public sector organizations, which might not have to deliver customer service at all. One police officer wrote us to tell about his struggle in providing customer service:

"Most of the public sector is in this monopoly position; if you are the victim of a crime, you *have* to use the local police, and so what benefit does huge investment in PR/satisfaction work yield? You, as a customer, can't go anywhere else. If you complain, you still get the same service you complained about, but a second time around. Our budget gets no bigger if we catch more criminals, and no smaller if we don't. Our income is generally guaranteed, so what is the loss if service is poor? Many forces and a lot of the public sector strive to be excellent/centers of excellence and are committed to lots of wonderful things. But why should we not just strive to perform at an acceptable level?"

So what about **Myth #7: Ethics, pride, and altruism are all legitimate reasons for providing customer service?**

Companies that are sustainable long-term are in business to make a profit on the products and services they provide. Every decision should be made with this in mind, including decisions about customer service. That isn't to say that ethics, pride, and possibly altruism don't play a part, but they are not the foundation of a *BAM!-good* customer service plan.

The Ethics Argument: Businesses are ethically or socially bound to give good customer service

The ethics argument goes like this: When a customer buys your product in good faith and pays hard-earned money for it, you are ethically obligated to provide the service to support that product and ensure that the customer can use it. If the product doesn't work or if it breaks, you, as the provider of the product, are obligated to replace it or fix it. This is straightforward, right? Statements like these are hard to argue with; after all, who would ever say they don't want to behave ethically? The answer, hopefully, is no one, as long as they are telling the truth.

Ethical standards by definition are unwavering. If an action is the ethical thing to do, it is ethical under all circumstances. Therefore, the standard of ethics isn't whether or not a company delivers good customer service or even whether a company delivers products that work. The measure of ethics is whether or not the company keeps its commitments in an honest and trustworthy way.

What is ethical under all circumstances is delivering on the service and capability that the company has committed to the customer— either overtly in the form of product specifications, service-level agreements, or warranty, or less directly in terms of advertising or promotional promises.

Ethical companies make only the commitments and promises that they intend to and are able to keep; therefore, assuming that a company must provide a certain level of customer service that has not been committed to the customer because it is somehow automatically ethical to do so is not a sustainable assumption. The ethical company will determine the characteristics of customer service product by product, service by service, based on the value that the company receives in return for that level of performance, and will determine their promises and commitments accordingly.

Ethical companies will consider the possibility of good and bad economic times when they make commitments to their customers. When times are flush or competition is keen, there is a risk of overpromising levels of service that may become financially painful or even impossible in times of economic downturn.

Ethical companies plan accordingly, and when they find that they must modify the commitments they have made to their customers, they communicate with the customer that the agreement between the company and the customer has changed, and will offer the customer a way to opt out of their service.

Ethical companies only make commitments that are in line with their economic goals for customers. They communicate with their customers and keep commitments. The customer then understands what she can expect and can opt in or out of doing business with the company.

The Pride Argument: We should provide customer service to promote our own individual sense of pride in a job well done

We want to have pride in our work. Part of that pride is keeping customers happy and satisfied. This is a nice thought and it may even make it to a motivational poster that you can hang in the break room at your company. However, pride isn't enough to sustain the delivery of customer service.

Pride is a feeling that comes and goes and is different from person to person. There is no way a company can define a standard feeling of pride for each of its employees. On a very difficult day, pride will crumble into many pieces. On these days, most of us just want to go home and forget about pride or anything else associated with our company. Pride is too fragile and varies too much from person to person to be used as a cornerstone for a customer service system. Pride cannot be a standard.

The Altruism Argument: Companies provide customer service because they intrinsically care about others

We believe that many people, companies included, want to do good by doing good. We want to help people. But when we are talking about customer service, the word "service" throws us off—as if there is something altruistic about taking care of customers. It isn't altruistic at all. A business takes care of its customers because it is in business to sell products or services for a price that people will pay and that produces an acceptable return to the company.

There is nothing altruistic about taking care of customers or about the standards of customer service we set. For-profit businesses are not altruistic. They exist to create financial returns to their shareholders by delivering on the expectations of participants and customers. Altruism can be an additional factor in business—but only because it is good for business in some bottom-line way. The triple-net bottom line is a way to evaluate corporate performance by measuring profits, environmental sustainability, and social responsibility.

The reason to provide *BAM!-good* customer service is because it increases the bottom line

We should not think about customer service as taking care of customers. We should think about it as one more feature of the product or service that we sell. We should think about it in terms of the commitment we made to our customers and in terms of how much value it adds to our business. The reason a company chooses to deliver *BAM!-good* customer service is because it will make more money by doing it.

Pull out your company's financial statements. Observe the lines that say cash, accounts receivable, and good will on the balance sheet. Stare at the net income line on your profit-and-loss statement. Providing customer service is only about building a profitable and sustainable company. Businesses pursue customer service because owners know that this creates revenue, reduces risk, and increases the probability of long-term sustainability.

This doesn't mean that we don't feel great affection for and interest in our customers. We must initially feel that way to build enduring relationships with them. But the basis of those relationships is economic—the value that the business provides to the customer in return for the money the customer pays.

Just like every other decision in business, we invest in customer service to get a tangible return or at least an intangible benefit. The first step in building the appropriate customer service plan is to establish the value of a customer.

A business may want to service all its customers excellently and equally, but it won't have the funds to do this unless it first serves the most valuable customers. Why? Because the volume and steadiness of the most valuable customers typically provide the resources for everything else the company does. But how do we figure out who those most valuable customers are, and more specifically calculate the economic value of a customer?

- Is it the revenue the customer generates?

- Is it the timing of that revenue?

- Is it the referrals they provide?

- Is it a service they provide that is complementary to ours?

- Is it the potential to sell add-on services to the company, its subsidiaries, or suppliers?

- Is it feedback they provide that helps the company improve its products or services?

- Is it the customer's brand, stature, or leadership in the marketplace that gives our company additional credibility?

Or is the value of a customer something less positive?

- The avoidance of word-of-mouth damage

- The public impact of losing customers to the competition

- The avoidance of negative Internet feedback

- The avoidance of lawsuits

Remember each of these reasons as we develop the thought process and a model that you can use to determine the economic value of each of your customers.

Revenue: The first measure of *BAM!-good* customer service

There are many other ways that customers add value to a company, but the starting point is annual revenue. For any company, regardless of size, industry, or distribution strategy, the first step in measuring the economic value of a customer is to determine how much money each customer spends with your company in a year.

Understanding how much revenue a customer produces for your company and the timing of that revenue provides a basis for figuring out how much you can or want to invest in customer service to retain and grow that customer. The objective is to create a reasonable model of the individual sources of company revenues as granularly as possible without getting buried in the detail.

Remember the basis for *BAM!-good* customer service is:

Attitude: There is an appropriate and healthy relationship between the revenue a customer generates for your business and the level of customer service you provide.

Action: Tracking revenue by customer is one of the building blocks of customer service, and the more granular the better.

Eric and Jennifer Warden use customer loyalty programs to reward repeat car wash and lube center customers. They track how much each customer spends on which Mustang Elite services as a way to determine how to best reward each individual customer. A customer who is a monthly regular for the top-of-the-line wash package might prefer a coupon for 20 percent off a complete detail job than a book of quickie washes. A customer who never buys a car wash but comes in every sixty days for an oil change at least once a year will likely appreciate a free quart of oil.

A rewards system serves the business, too, by collecting the information that allows a company to understand who does the most business with the company. Thinking about how much money an individual customer spends with your company helps crystallize the concept of the economic value of a customer. In industries that follow a subscription model, this way of framing the value of keeping or losing a customer is the basis for programs that are designed to prevent churn.

In the early nineties, Mary Jane was vice-president of sales and marketing for ARDIS, an early entrant into the wireless data networking business. ARDIS customers used mobile devices that were linked to massive legacy computer applications for field service and sales reporting. It usually took a customer a year to eighteen months and a budget of a $1 million or more to implement the system, but they invested, because once the system was operational, their payback was significant.

ARDIS followed the mobile voice and data revenue model that is nearly ubiquitous with wireless carriers today—the customer paid a registration fee and then a fixed or variable usage charge every month. In a business model like this, it is fairly easy to calculate the revenue benefit of a single user. With ARDIS, companies registered from 600 to 3,000 or more users on the network on multi-year agreements that ranged from $60 to $150 or more per user per month, which totaled from $2,000 to $5,000 or more over thirty-six months. When a user had a problem or concern, ARDIS understood exactly what the company would be losing if it didn't solve that user's problem.

It's the same with cellular telephone carriers. When the user who never uses up all the minutes in her plan, doesn't want a paper bill, and pays promptly every month through automatic debit calls in with a problem, the customer service rep usually offers some concession. Why? Because companies like Verizon and AT&T understand how much revenue every single customer generates. Do you?

Imagine your best customer. How much revenue does that customer generate in a year? Knowing what you know about the business that customer has produced for you, how much would you be willing to invest to keep that customer or to attract a dozen more like her?

Do you know the cost of every customer?

To produce *BAM!-good* customer service that drops to the bottom line, a company needs to understand how profitable each of its revenue-generating customers is. A customer could generate a lot of revenue, but there also may be a lot of cost to support them. Every aspect of dealing with a customer adds to the cost of doing business with them.

What about revenue timing?

When and how a customer pays can be as important as how much they pay. But not all cash is created equal. If a customer prepays an invoice ninety days in advance, it has an obvious positive cash impact on your company. If a customer pays late, it costs more to service that customer, because not only do you have the cost of goods sold for the actual transaction, but you need to invest administrative staff time to chase payment for that revenue.

Many banks and mortgage processors during the Great Recession of 2008-2009 realized that while they were good at accepting mostly on-time payments, they did not have the infrastructure in place to collect late payments from a very large number of homeowners. This crushed the infrastructure of even the mightiest institutions. Alternately, if a customer buys during a slow period of your business (e.g., they are a counter-cyclical customer), this may be more beneficial to you than if you are a retailer and they buy at Christmas.

How important are referrals and buzz?

As long as a business has excess capacity, customer referrals are a good thing. Satisfied customers tend to tell other people in their lives about services and products they like. Think about how you make decisions on everything from plumbers to real estate agents to which television or computer you buy.

Customers—whether they are individual consumers or company-types—tend to talk to and associate with people with similar interests, lifestyles, and occupations. If a customer has the profile that is desirable to a business, then it only makes sense to try to attract others with similar profiles. Eric and Jenny Warden's Mustang Elite customer loyalty program rewards customers for referring other people to the car wash. An average customer who washes her car once a week and changes oil every three months spends more than $1,000 a year with Mustang Elite, and that's before she purchases gift items, gum, or bottled water at the register.

So does that mean that every referral is worth $1,000 a year? No. But it does show that every referral is worth something, and the value of that something is measurable and tangible. It is the ultimate multiplier effect every business needs to be successful. For most businesses, it is not economically possible to acquire a person from "scratch" through advertising and other marketing campaigns. It becomes too expensive. If you can get your customers talking about you and get a trusted referral to your business, the cost for that new customer decreases and makes your business more profitable. This multiplier effect is the cornerstone of every multilevel marketing business where you invite your friends to buy from you and they invite their friends. Today, it is also the cornerstone of any social media plan (think Facebook, LinkedIn, and Twitter) where the people you are connected to talk about you to the people they are connected to. It has worked millions of times.

Unfortunately, it can also work the other way. Remember **Myth #10: Unhappy customers tell their stories to more people than happy customers do.**

 Happy and unhappy customers both tell their stories. Neutral customers likely don't talk much about your company at all. The bottom line is which stories would you rather have told?

Manish Patel, CEO of Where 2 Get It, told us that the multiplier effect of unsatisfied customers is even worse with today's technology. "If you have a bad experience, you might tell ten people, but today you can tell ten million people. They can take a quick YouTube video, do a podcast, virally send it out, and you and the brand won't understand what hit you, but when one person has that power, it's important to provide what they want."

Not every customer will tell you honestly what he or she thinks of your company or product. Typically, the people who write and call you are the ones who are really upset or really happy. You need to find a way to listen to all of these people and to get the customers who never say anything to talk. These customers are valuable because they will tell you things that you are unable to learn being inside the company. Many times, if a few customers are thinking something, there are a lot of other customers you never hear from who suffer in silence but are thinking the same thing. Something can be done about unhappy customers.

Remember **Myth #11: Unhappy customers are a part of doing business. If you handle a customer complaint well, the offended customer will turn around and be an even more loyal customer.**

 There is a tremendous cost to any business of dealing with an unhappy customer. They make more phone calls. It takes time and human resources to deal with them—and deep down, think about it. When a company makes a customer feel dissatisfied—remember Mary Jane's American Airlines Admirals Club experience?—can that company ever completely undo that feeling in the customer? The jury is out on this, but would you really want to take the chance?

Unhappy customers do not have to be a part of doing business. It costs more in the long run to handle a customer complaint—and customers never entirely forget.

This is not the way to run a company. The goal is to prevent customer service issues before they even start. Apologies for bad customer service are fine. But they are just that, apologies, and don't ever really take the sting away from the error.

Retention and stickiness

How likely is your customer to remain with you even if you screw up servicing them? Some customers have more tolerance with one-time mistakes than others. It usually depends on the loyalty you have built up with the customer up to that point, or the laziness the customer has in switching to another vendor. While this factor is difficult to measure, it is good to track whether the customer leaves after a bad incident. Understanding exactly when the customer exited will give your company information on what your customers consider "fatal" mistakes.

Riding your customer's brand

Brands are a powerful thing in the marketplace, and they influence market share. One of the first things a new business wants to do is to find a large, powerful company with a great brand to buy and then talk about that success. The thought process goes that if Microsoft or Coca-Cola (or some other very powerful brand) thinks my company's product or service is the best, then it must be! This "success by association" is why many smaller companies put logos of familiar companies on their Web sites, to instill confidence in prospects that this is someone who can be trusted for business.

A powerful brand can be much more valuable to a company as a customer than the amount of revenue they produce. Suppose Microsoft bought one copy of this book and mentioned it, and the local chain of dry cleaner bought one hundred. As much as we like our local dry cleaner and would appreciate the sale, Microsoft's one copy may be more valuable in attracting new customers than the revenue from the dry cleaner. The international Microsoft brand acts as a multiplier and a trusted agent to make it cost-effective to attract new customers.

Quantitative calculation of the value of a customer

Once you know what a customer is worth to your business, you know what to invest in *BAM!-good* customer service to get or retain one. We have developed a formula to calculate what a customer is worth to you. This is a series of categories and relative point values that you can assign to your customer base. We recommend you use our example as a guide for your company. The categories and the point counts are not intended to be absolute, but to be used as a guideline.

Customer Value Calculation

Each of your customers will have a weighted score of 1 to 22.

<u>Revenue</u>: What is the customer's rank in terms of revenue?

- Bottom 25% - add **1 point**
- Bottom 50% - add **2 points**
- Top 50% - add **3 points**
- Top 25% - add **4 points**

<u>Timing (add **2 points**)</u>: What is this client's accounts receivable history? Do they pay on time? In cash/by check/by credit card?

<u>Referrals (add **4 points**)</u>: Have they ever referred any new prospects to you? Did that person do business with you? Did that person refer someone else?

<u>Additional products they buy (add **3 points**)</u>: Does this client purchase additional products or services from you? Could they in the future? What would be the dollar value of these sales?

<u>Feedback they give you (add **1 point**)</u>: Does this client tell you how they feel about doing business with you before they are unhappy enough to complain—verbally, on surveys, on comment cards, on the Web?

<u>Stickiness (add **2 points**)</u>: Have they been your customer for more than two years?

<u>Brand power (add **4 points**)</u>: Do you have a competitive edge with this customer?

<u>Unhappy customer (subtract **2 points**)</u>: Has this customer ever been unhappy with you? Have they ever complained? Have any of your employees ever complained about them?

The following two clients are of equal value to your company, but in different ways.

Example 1: Customer A is one of your best clients. They always pay on time and give you many referrals. They only buy your top product, never give you feedback, and they have been with you for a long time. They are not a major brand.

Revenue	Top 25%	+ 4 points
Timing of Payments	On Time	+ 2 points
Referrals	Yes, often	+ 4 points
Additional Products	No	0 points
Feedback	No	0 points
Stickiness	Yes	+ 2 points
Brand Power	No	0 points
Unhappy Customer	No	0 points
Total Value		**12 points**

Example 2: Customer B is an important client but not your top customer. They typically pay on time, and they give you no referrals or feedback. They do buy many of your products, and they are a major-brand company. However, your company shipped them the wrong products a year ago, and they were very upset about it. They have continued to do business with you.

Revenue	Top 50%	+ 3 points
Timing of Payments	On Time	+ 2 points
Referrals	No	0 points
Additional Products	Yes	+ 3 points
Feedback	No	0 points
Stickiness	Yes	+ 2 points
Brand Power	Yes	+ 4 points
Unhappy Customer	Yes	- 2 points
Total Value		**12 points**

Revenue: It is always important to know how much business a customer does with you by volume and by the money they spend. Are they number 1 or number 4,321? While this may be a measure of their satisfaction, it is also a measure of how well your company solves their problems or, less favorably, a measure that your company hasn't done something so terribly wrong to get them so angry that they want to complain and switch to another vendor. Under the category of "no news is good news," a customer who keeps spending money with you demonstrates a certain measure of satisfaction, but not a guarantee.

How to measure satisfaction from this customer: Ask them why they buy the level or quantity of goods or services from you that they do. Don't be afraid to do this.

Timely Bill Payment: This may or may not be a measure of satisfaction. People pay bills based on personal habits, needs, and cash flow. The customer you are serving directly may not be the person who pays the bills. There may be company standards for paying that are longer than you would like. Economic realities sometimes move the payment of all vendors to 90 to 120 days. A *BAM!-good* customer is not necessarily one who pays on time, but one who pays consistently in a time frame that you can count on for your cash flow.

How to measure satisfaction from this customer: You can measure their satisfaction by monitoring their payment behavior. If they have been consistently paying their bills on time and things change, this may be an indication of a change in their level of satisfaction with your product, or it could be a change in their financial situation. Either way, call the customer to find out what is really going on.

Referrals: Companies want and expect satisfied customers to talk about the company and to refer other business to you. But satisfied customers don't always talk. There are "sneezers" who constantly tell other people when they are satisfied or dissatisfied with a product.[5] But there are other very satisfied customers who actually never say anything to anyone. They are satisfied but just are not sneezers or talkers.

How to measure satisfaction from this customer: Proactively ask if they would refer someone to you. Be active in your solicitation of new leads. A meeting with Barry's insurance agent never goes by where the agent does not ask him for a referral. (If you can use more insurance, please contact Dana Potts at Northwestern Mutual Life.) You can turn everyone into a referral source for you. This is also the best way to find new customers, because you have a current customer as the bridge to establishing credibility with a prospect.

Additional Product: Does this customer buy more than one product or service from you? Do you offer additional products and services that they could buy from you but purchase from someone else?

How to measure satisfaction from this customer: Schedule an appointment specifically to talk about the full range of products and services that you provide. Ask them if any of those fit needs they already have. If you discover they are buying something you sell from someone else, determine how much they are spending a year. Ask them if you could be competitive, would they do that business with you. If they say no, you know you have a problem.

Feedback: Again, some of your customers are communicators and some are not. This is not necessarily a measure of their satisfaction. It is proven that people who are really satisfied and really dissatisfied talk the most. They send you either rave letters or complaints. Ask for feedback in a neutral manner if you really want to hear what people have to say.

How to measure satisfaction from this customer: The tools are not simple and can be biased. (See Chapter 6.)

Stickiness: This is an important metric. But again, it really is an indication that you either have not done something so terribly wrong or that your competition has not done something right enough to make your customers want to switch. It is not an indication of *BAM!-good* satisfaction. Most consumers are a lazy bunch, and they stay with companies where they are mostly satisfied to slightly dissatisfied all the time. It does take a lot for a consumer to change, since in many services there are costs and penalties associated with any change. For example, how many times have you disliked your cellular phone service but were too lazy to switch? What about your attorney or accountant? Consumers are creatures of habit.

How to measure satisfaction from this customer: Ask them why they continue to be your customer. Ask them if they have ever wanted to do business with someone else instead of you, and if so why.

Brand Power: As discussed above, your company can ride the coattails of a well-recognized brand.

How to measure satisfaction from this customer: Ask permission to use them as a reference or to use their logo on your Web site or in marketing materials.

Unhappy Customer: This customer has expressed their unhappiness and dissatisfaction.

How to measure satisfaction from this customer: After the event, ask them every six months if they are satisfied. Give them extra attention and ask them if it is making a difference. Remember, it takes time and effort on the part of the company to help a customer feel good again.

Busting the myths that can confuse a company's measure of customer value

To adopt the value-proposition approach to customer service that we have been talking about in this chapter, a company must bust **Myth #8: If you learn how to "put up with your customers," business will be great!**

Just "putting up with" the customers never made anyone's business great. Businesses are great *because* we have customers and they pay us real dollars for our goods and services, not because they are interruptions or annoyances that we have learned to tolerate. This attitude is a recipe for slow death of a business. We once saw a poster that should probably be hanging in this type of company: *"If we don't take care of the customer, maybe they will stop bothering us!"*[6]

Hard to believe, but there are many people in business who see customers as a necessary evil. If the slogan on this poster reflects your silent wish, cheer up—you will probably get your wish. A company and its employees can't have this much disdain for customers and still stay in business for very long.

Every business needs both customers and prospects. If the goal is to turn prospects into customers, it makes no sense to have different levels of customer service for both. So much for **Myth #9: Taking care of the customers you have is more important than getting new customers.**

Once a company quantifies that customer service creates value, you want to start creating that value with a qualified prospect as soon as you can.

It is certainly true that the highest cost of sales is almost always in finding and closing new customers. However, a company might be in a business where new customers are absolutely necessary. At some point, every business needs new customers. Take the extreme example—the funeral home business.

Mary Jane grew up in a small town where her family has lived for several generations. Since the early 1900s, her family always used the same funeral home family to bury their dead. While the courtesy and care of the deceased family is unfailing, the Nunnelee Funeral Home team is just as caring and focused on the mourners who aren't in the family. Think about it—every single person in town is a person they could eventually serve.

The ultimate situation is to have customers who are so happy with your products and services that they ask you what else you are selling that they might be able to buy from you. Many companies pursue a strategy of selling additional items to the customers they have, since conventional wisdom says that it is easier to sell more things to a customer you have than land a new customer. This is only true if the type of customers you have can be integrated horizontally and are in a position to buy more things from you.

For example, cable companies at one point just sold cable television services. Then they decided to use the same cable coming to your house to compete with the telephone company and the Internet service provider (ISP) to sell telephone and Internet services. They even started provided discounted packages if you bought all three. A customer is inclined to go with one vendor if they are initially satisfied with them on the first product, if the vendor adds a financial incentive to bundle more products or services, or if the customer is even slightly dissatisfied with the other vendor. Having customers who can buy other things from you makes them valuable and profitable, but they need to be satisfied with the first thing you sold them (and get great customer service).

But at some point, existing customers are customers no more. Maybe they relocate, stop needing what you sell, find a higher quality and lower-cost alternative from your competitor, become dissatisfied with your company or products, or they simply want to try something new. This is going to happen.

This is why it isn't an either/or situation when a company prioritizes customer service for prospects and customers. The customer service attitudes (for sure), and actions (as far as they apply) that you put in place for an existing customer should apply equally to your prospects. If you aren't willing to do that or can't afford to do that, it is likely that the person you are thinking of as a prospect isn't going to materialize into the profitable customer you want anyway.

To deliver *BAM!-good* customer service, a company must put a value on each customer. While this may sound cold, there is nothing heartless about basing a business relationship on an economic decision. Once the company has decided that the economics of *BAM!-good* customer service make sense, Chapter 4 helps identify the barriers to delivery.

Chapter 4:
Why Don't We Deliver the Customer Service We Say We Want to Deliver?

Every mission statement from every company in the world includes giving "good" customer service. If this is part of every mission, why do so many companies fail so miserably? Why do customers get frustrated and so angry? If we accept that good customer service is important, why don't we do what it takes to help our customers feel satisfied? Is it us or is it them? What prevents us from accomplishing this goal?

"Help line" columns are popular features in many newspapers and magazines. Most of us know how it works because we read these columns regularly. Readers write in and describe the problems they are having with companies. The "problem solver" contacts the company and many times gets the problem resolved. We read every one of these columns—especially since writing this book—and we never fail to shake our heads in disbelief.

After being contacted by the "help line," the offending company almost always ends up resolving the problem the way the customer would have wanted it resolved in the first place. In many cases, the company goes well beyond what the customer was originally asking for. We always wonder why a company wouldn't have done that when the customer first called. Were they forced into an eleventh-hour public relations play to minimize the bad press in the column? Or is it—as we would prefer to think—that the company's process for resolving customer issues broke down and that once they had visibility to their customer's concern, they were willing to solve the problem in a reasonable way?

Christopher Elliott, who writes the popular ombudsman column for *National Geographic Traveler* and other magazines[7], is not so optimistic. "An increasing number of companies ignore my requests," he says, "believing that if they don't respond (or wait long enough), I'll go away. That tends to backfire, because if the problem is severe enough, I'll blog about it, even if they don't answer."

Elliott tells us that his success rate in resolving issues is about 66 percent. "It's difficult to say if the company wants to avoid a public relations nightmare, or if it just wants to do the right thing," he says. "I'm willing to give them the benefit of the doubt. Having said that, my sense is that there are more companies out there that regard customer service as just another thing to be outsourced. It's not part of their company DNA. I think that's a dangerous way to think about something that should really be a part of everything that you do."

Roadblocks to customer service are both systemic and situational

If the mission of delivering good customer service had easy solutions, everyone would be doing it. Some obstacles are put on companies from outside forces they can't control, but businesses also create many of these problems for themselves. Certainly, there are plenty of obstacles to good customer service that are caused by our actions and our attitudes. Often problems appear when well-intended companies move too fast—perhaps making a change to respond to market or economic conditions without thoroughly considering the potential impact on all customers.

We call the roadblocks to delivering excellent customer service *Bam!* **Blockers**. They fall into three categories:

1. Beliefs, lamentations, and excuses block the delivery of good customer service.

2. Preventable actions and attitudes can impair customer service.

3. Unpreventable challenges to customer service can occur when the business isn't prepared to counteract their effect.

Beliefs, lamentations, and excuses block the delivery of good customer service

First, just a reminder of the fundamental premise of this book: The definition of *BAM!-good* customer service is those actions and attitudes that a business takes and holds that help a customer *feel* more satisfied. If a business cannot accept and believe this, then delivering *BAM!-good* customer service will be a very bumpy road and likely won't lead to the desired destination of increased profitability.

Before we identify the *BAM! Blockers* to good customers service, we need to bust the customer service myths that relieve us from the responsibility of offering *BAM!-good* customer service. Consider **Myth #12: Customers don't care about great service; they just want**

the lowest price possible and **Myth #14: Forget about customer service; people buy from those they like**.

First, let's talk about low cost and low price. More and more in this world—especially with the advent of the personalized service that is being delivered cost-effectively over the Internet—customers expect low prices and great customer service. Low price in return for low service was an escape for the early airline discounter Southwest Airlines and the pioneer in customer warehouse selling Costco. But neither of these successful businesses really ever provided bad customer experiences. Instead, they set and then delivered on customer expectations, even making the "less is more" concept part of their brands.

Certainly there may well be economic factors that get in the way of our businesses doing all that we would like to do in the way of customer service. Resource limitations challenge everything a business tries to accomplish—why would we expect customer service to be any different? But when it comes to adding that next *BAM!-good* new hire or finding the dollars for an Internet ad that we believe will show results, companies find the money. It should be the same with customer service. There are many approaches to customer service that don't add significantly to incremental cost or price.

For example, characterizing, recording, and tracking customers' problems enables a business to recognize and resolve problems so the next set of customers aren't affected by them. Depending on the size of the organization, this can be implemented with simple spreadsheet tools and reviewed by management.

As for the myth that people buy from people they like, it is probably true that people will not buy from people they intensely dislike. It also is true that some people like the people they buy from. But what is always true is that people buy from people who help them feel satisfied.

Tackling the *BAM!* Blockers

BAM! Blocker #1: Our company's economic model works only if front-line customer positions pay minimum wage.

There is a common complaint among owners and managers: "I can't afford to hire people who can perform." Owners lament that they can't expect the employee they attract with minimum wage to deliver customer service and be the person with the capabilities that the customer wants on the other end of the telephone line when they call in.

Many American companies say they are economically forced to base their customer service operations in other countries to make them affordable. Yet, from our real-life experience or intuitively, we as customers know that this simply isn't true.

As we have seen in the economic downturn of 2008 and 2009 in the financial sector, being paid a lot of money does not guarantee higher performance. Similarly, we have seen a lot of people making $6 to $7 per hour turn in great performances. The point is that we need to hire the right person for the right job. We may have to pay more to get a better-performing employee for certain situations, but we don't have to start there. Online retailer Zappos is known for not paying the most for their customer service jobs, but manages to get their people to deliver great service. [8]

The starting point is with the CEO who sets the standard that every person hired owns the delivery of customer service for their area or location for the entire time they are on the job. A process that starts this way will be bolstered and improved with the appropriate investment in hiring—to find individuals who have the attitude that matches this type of environment—and training so that these individuals are equipped to know what actions to take with customers.

Susan Landa of The Fossil Cartel tells us, "We hire extroverted people; people with good people skills, a pleasant personality; they look at you when they talk to you. I also look for a basic knowledge of rocks; however, I would hire personality over knowledge of rocks. When I'm interviewing them, I tell them what the job entails—breaking the ice with people, schmoozing—and I give them a handbook, and as they work the first few days in the store, they're taken minute by minute and they get their practice greeting customers, and after thirty days I do a review, and I'll explain what needs to be improved or praise them."

To illustrate the point, for as many bad customer service experiences as we have in retail and fast food environments, think of the good examples. Wal-Mart understands. When was the last time you walked into a Wal-Mart that you were not greeted? It is no accident that the geniuses in Arkansas teach their store managers to hire retired people as greeters—people you might imagine have long histories of being customers and perhaps serving them; people who have an attitude of respect and the motivation to connect with others.

With Wal-Mart's success in this area, "greeter" now has become an official position in other retail stores, such as GAP, Target, Menard's, and Abercrombie & Fitch.

In Japan, customers are greeted with *irrashaimase*, which means "welcome," when they step inside a store, restaurant, or someone's section in a department store. Another nice touch in Japan is that every effort is made to give and receive objects with two hands. In many retail stores in Japan, the salesperson will come around from the counter and hand the customer the shopping bag, which has been taped closed, and will bow. The customer (if they are Japanese) will accept with two hands and bow back. Sometimes more bows are exchanged (and many thank-yous—thank you for buying, thank you for your help), and the sales representative will bow deeply as the customer leaves the store. If there is a line or the sales person is behind a long counter, they won't come around, but the bowing is always there. If they don't bow you out of the store, another salesperson will. All the salespeople who aren't busy will bow and thank you for your patronage. Is this strictly a cultural behavior? We don't think so. When Barry bought something in a store in Japan, he honestly felt as if the person selling it to him appreciated his business and even appreciated his stopping in the store, whether he bought something or not.

We've noticed that more places—mostly in clothing retail—are handing bags with both hands, held so that the customer can easily grasp the handles. We have also seen hotel chains like Marriott and car rental companies like Enterprise come around to the customer's side of the counter to complete the transaction. This is a small gesture that anyone can do and costs nothing. It helps the customer feel appreciated.

Susan Landa also thinks that good salesmanship is part of good customer service "because in a salesman's role, you have to be able to read a customer, read their body cues, their energy, when to step in and when to step back. I call it the sales dance, because with one person you might do a tango and with another you might do a jig. In the end it's about the customer's experience—if they're there to look, they're there to look—give them some information so they can have an informative experience."

BAM! Blocker #2: The computer or support system I have stinks.

Managers and front-line workers lament that the computer systems, telephone systems, or other support elements do not support good customer service, or "that's the way our computer does it." Sometimes this is certainly the case. Systems can be cumbersome or outdated, or can use data that is just plain wrong.

This is further complicated by **Myth #17: Customer service systems should focus on trouble shooting. If it isn't broken, don't fix it.**

 Just because no one is complaining (yet) doesn't mean things are working as well as they could. In fact, no matter how wonderful or terrible these systems are, you can bet that the people who use them every day have appropriate ideas and suggestions for how to use them better—including ideas that wouldn't cost a bundle to implement.

Every business needs to find a way to collect this input, discuss it, and take appropriate actions to leverage whatever tools and systems they have in place. Improvements need to be identified by the front-line staff and communicated to the management team. Small changes in support systems can make a difference.

For example, sophisticated computer systems can certainly identify the last time a customer called or visited and what their issue was. However, simply training the staff in what it means and how to provide excellent customer service will trump any fancy computer system.

For Zappos, the online retailer, there is no monitoring of call times and no scripts. Call center reps have so much power, it's critical to make sure they're a cultural fit. To do that, CEO Tony Hsieh reportedly offers new customer service agents $2,000 to leave the company after an initial training period if the new hires don't think they mesh with Zappos's zany culture.[9]

BAM! Blocker #3: Customers are fundamentally unreasonable people who set out to prey on business owners, nicking away at profitability by asking for more than they are willing to pay for.

Some customers are unreasonable; most are not. With a belief like this, a business owner will always, always, always encounter obstacles in delivering *BAM!-good* customer service. The only solution is to change this attitude or fire the customers who are making you or your employees feel this way. Once a business understands the value that each customer contributes to the bottom line based on revenue over cost, it will know if there are customers who need to be fired. No business needs every potential customer. In Chapter 7, we discuss when and how to fire those customers.

A dangerous flip side to the quote above is **Myth # 19: You can satisfy all of the customers all of the time.**

There is a belief that if a company invests enough, trains enough, asks enough questions, listens enough, and really, really cares, all customers can be satisfied all the time. This is impossible. By pretending that this is true, a company can actually create more of a customer issue, and it can certainly be demoralizing to employees if we set a goal that can never be reached.

BAM! Blocker #4: We believe in setting high goals and standards for our company, and higher expectations for our customers, whether we can deliver on those goals and expectations or not.

This happens when a company's leadership bases the reason for customer service on something other than marginal revenue and profit. We've talked already about pride, altruism, and morals as positive characteristics for human behavior, but not appropriate foundations for customer service. Neither is stating goals to make a public relations point without a matching commitment to deliver or in an effort to differentiate your company from a competitor.

Customers and desirable prospects will base their expectations on the expectations that a business or its competitors set. If your business doesn't plan to treat all customers in all circumstances with respect, don't create a tagline that suggests you value them. Don't set customer service goals they can't achieve with the people and resources you have. Goals need to be set that are financially integrated into the business and can be achieved by the current support structure and staff.

In one of Barry's own companies, they set a goal to answer every phone call within fifteen seconds. This goal became unprofitable. Customers were willing to wait when the company set a longer expectation for how long they would be on the phone. The company set customer expectations appropriately.

By examining how long the wait queues are in your customer service center and the call abandonment rate (how often people hang up without talking to someone), you will be able to staff to the appropriate levels based on affordable hold times. This is different from the experience that you can have when you call cable provider Comcast. They force you to listen to multiple commercials about their products while you are on hold!

Preventable actions impair customer service

There are practices and actions in every business that owners who are committed to *BAM!-good* customer service can eliminate, improve, anticipate, and fix.

Many times corrections have to do with the product or the way it is marketed, distributed, or supported. But don't get taken in by **Myth #4: Customer service is about having high-quality products.**

 *BAM!-good* customer service is about so much more than having high-quality products, and when companies rely only on the quality of their products to deliver customer service, they will end up with dissatisfied customers, no matter how great their products are.

Consider product features that in the past companies could use to close the customer service gap, which are now a requirement just to be in the marketplace.

- **Product quality.** There is so much choice out there today that if products don't work, we don't buy them. Even giants learn this the hard way—consider Microsoft and its Vista operating system. After a short time, new computer manufacturers were offering the older operating system, Windows XP, as an extra *cost upgrade*!

- **Product availability.** In the past, companies that had terrific logistics systems used to have a competitive advantage because their products were easier to find, order, replace, or refill than their competitors' products. Now with the proliferation of virtual stores on the Internet and outsourcing of distribution, companies can deliver terrific availability without investing in technology, warehouses, inventories, or trucks.

- **Usability.** Products have to be easy to use and intuitive. Gen X and Y buyers, as well as Baby Boomers, insist on it. There are lots of examples, from the screens, icons, and buttons on cellular phones—with the iPhone the most recent example.

- **Features/Functionality.** There is constant "one-upsmanship" in the marketplace. AT&T comes out with its 3G network, and six months later a competitor is touting its 4G.

BAM! Blocker #5: There is nothing we can do in customer service since our products in the marketplace are so far from perfect.

This can be temporary while the company is working through quality issues. It could be one product line among many, or the company may have decided that supplying a product that is "mostly" right is good enough. Identify these issues, make them known to the customers, tell them what you are doing about it (or what you aren't), and the time frame for resolution.

Saying that a company has decided to sell a product or service that is "just good enough" might go against the grain. Yet there are thousands of companies who follow that standard and successfully sell millions of products to people like you and us every day. The best product is not always the one that sells the best. That's because *BAM!-good* customer service can overcome many product deficiencies. Revenue is mostly tied to execution, marketing, and distribution. It really is not all about the product itself, but rather it is about how we execute its marketing and distribution to get prospects to be aware, to buy the product, and to be happy that they did.

Consider Microsoft. No one has ever accused this company of having amazing products. But from the start Microsoft built excellent marketing and distribution. The company was able to get their DOS and later Windows operating systems on most of the computers produced. As Microsoft has proven again and again, even if a product isn't better than the competition, if it has enough of the features and functionality people want, they will buy it when it is positioned properly, marketed heavily, and distributed broadly enough so it is easy to buy from a company that makes them feel satisfied.

BAM!-good customer service compensates for product features and quality. Customer service is of course made easier if people are delighted with your product. It is a lot easier to have a happy and satisfied customer who loves your product and now and then has a little problem that's easy to fix than to have a customer who hates your product because it consistently underperforms.

The dealers for Lexus, which is continuously rated as one of the best car brands in America, pump millions of dollars into the service end of their business. The local Lexus dealer, McGrath Lexus, revamped their service department with comfortable places to sit while you wait for your car. Besides free Wi-Fi, you can sip of cup of latte at the café. Your children can play at their own center while you practice on the indoor putting green. And, yes, McGrath washes your car on the way out. Is it the quality of the Lexus car that keeps customers coming back or is it the way they feel about Lexus service?

BAM! Blocker #6: The business believes it is delivering good customer service, when, from the customer perspective, clients are tolerating things.

How your customers really feel about doing business with your company definitely is not "all in the cards." **Myth #16: Comment cards and customer surveys accurately measure customer service.**

These types of feedback mechanisms only capture a small percentage of customers and only bits of their total reactions to your products and service. In the first place, many customers do not respond when they are satisfied. As time passes, they may feel little twinges of dissatisfaction. They start out being patient, move to tolerating something, move on to impatience, and then to dissatisfaction and anger.

The ticket taker may provide good service as passengers are loading the airplane, but the cabin attendant may be impolite or spend more time in the jump seat reading *People Magazine* than taking care of passengers. The feedback we receive may be influenced by when and how we ask for it.

BAM! Blocker #7: Just because the customers aren't mad doesn't mean you are delivering good customer service.

As customers, we can be a lazy bunch and do not want to take the initiative or go through the analysis it takes to switch vendors. Just because they are not complaining doesn't mean they are satisfied. Get to the issue before it becomes a revolt again by having feedback mechanisms in place at many stages of customer interaction.

BAM! Blocker #8: What was customer service yesterday may not be seen as good customer service today.

Maybe the company has gone through a growth spurt or a contraction, or maybe customer needs and desires have shifted. Perhaps the company is serving new or different people, or a competitor has redefined the playing field. MotiveQuest is a strategic-planning consultancy that studies customer motivations through analyzing online conversations. In 2007, a major department store chain was faced with an important issue. They were dropping in the influential *BusinessWeek* Service Rankings and wanted to know why. Traditional survey and focus group research had not yielded any answers, so MotiveQuest was asked to analyze the problem. When they examined seventeen million conversations from 937,000 different individuals, 13 percent had something to do with service. MotiveQuest then analyzed these 2.2 million messages to identify and understand the key drivers of service. They identified four key drivers of service: personal, trust, respect, and convenience. While personal was the least discussed driver, it is the most emotional and important. When the company looked at the traditional retail category, they saw that none of the retailers indexed highly on personal—so investments in this area could provide a sustainable competitive advantage. Personal is also the driver that has changed the most, since with the Internet, the emphasis is on personalization and customization. Online retailers refer to this as PEC, a "personal, emotional connection." Barry frequently stays at the Portland Paramount, not because it is the best hotel in town, but because he is remembered every time he returns.

Consumer expectations of service are changing rapidly, and retailers are not keeping up. For example, when you go to Amazon. com, the site remembers who you are and what you have purchased. Amazon makes recommendations based on your purchase history and tells you what other people like you buy. Amazon provides a community with reviews; stores your preferences; and provides a personalized, informed, customized shopping experience each time you visit. As a consumer, you have learned that these things are possible and you like them. We are less satisfied when we have a buying experience that doesn't include them. Unfortunately for bricks-and-mortar businesses, we buyers don't put on a different service hat when visiting a traditional retailer, so we wonder why they don't remember us, make recommendations, and personalize our service experience.

BAM! Blocker #9: Conditions have changed and the company cannot deliver the same level of customer service as before.

Maybe a competitor is paying more than you can, and they've hired your best people away. The general economic climate may have deteriorated in your industry. This is exactly why delivering *BAM!-good* customer service needs to be tied to the economic goals of the company.

BAM! Blocker #10: The basic prerequisites for customer service are missing. Stop using that cell phone!

A company must honestly care for and be passionate about its customers. There must be defined processes to provide *BAM!-good* customer service and to deal with dissatisfied customers. The thing that has helped and hurt customer service tremendously in this decade has been the ubiquitous cell phone. Everyone uses them, on and off the job. While cell phones offer the potential to provide great responsiveness to customers with the ability to get back to them 24/7, they also interfere and distract employees from focusing on their jobs. With the ability to have short conversations or send text messages, cell phones hurt the employees' ability to keep their attention on the customer as their first priority. How many times have you seen a post office delivery person on their cell phone while she is delivering the mail or a security officer in a commercial building texting from his cell phone while "watching the building," or a taxi driver taking a call while driving you to your destination? All the time, right? We have even eyed TSA officers on their cell phones while screening travelers! Every company needs to set strict guidelines on when and where cell phones can be used.

Tracey Welsh, the general manager at Red Mountain Spa in Utah, told us, "Cell phones are a problem in people delivering excellent customer service. We don't want that cell phone to ruin the guest experience. Technology overall has been necessary to keep business growing. Unfortunately, when e-mail came to the hotel industry, it put people in their offices and not out on the floor. As small as we are, we find ourselves guilty of it."

BAM! Blocker #11: The company leadership is saying one thing about customer service, but acting a different way.

The company is setting expectations that don't match what they are economically able to deliver. Management speaks derogatorily about customers in private, but says something else different publicly. Employees will always mirror the actions and attitudes of the company leadership, no matter what words are stated publicly.

Deborah House, CEO of the Adare Group, told us, "Good customer service to me means not that you never make a mistake, but that you correct it quickly. So I guess, in my world, I expect everyone to mess up—I do it every hour—but I expect them to fix it quickly and to not argue with me. So I think it's all in the fix, not in the initial mistake. It means actually delivering what you're advertising."

BAM! Blocker #12: Employees don't like their jobs. They kick the cat, taking their frustration out on the customers.

There is no release valve for employees to express their frustrations and not take it out on the customer (or proverbially kick the cat when they get home). Feedback methods for employees are just as important as those in place for customers. Wouldn't it be great if companies had an isolated room just for employees to scream and vent their frustrations about difficult customers?

BAM! Blocker #13: The company doesn't train employees with the specifics of satisfying customers.

The company does not tell the employees what is expected of them or the goals in relation to customer service. Again, tailored training for employees facing customers is critical. Employees will treat customers the way the company teaches them to treat customers. Some people take to it more readily, but if your company subscribes to **Myth #15: There are people who are naturally good at customer service**; the company is going to have some very unhappy customers.

 Most humans are not born with the desire or knowledge to deliver good customer service. It doesn't come automatically—especially in today's egalitarian, self-service world. Train them!

Carl Albrecht, CEO at PointManagement, LLC, says, "I think the biggest obstacle has been that, even though it is what we do, it's hard to put my personality into people, it's hard to drive the kind of bias for action and getting really excited about customer service down to every last person. Does it scale? Yes, I think so, I think it's an important thing, but it's hard. I read something, maybe it was a Tom Peters–type thing, 'Every time I call up your company, they are so friendly, and how do you get them to be so friendly?' 'Well, we hire friendly people.' So in interviews, if they aren't enthusiastic or they don't come out of their shell, then we don't hire them."

BAM! Blocker #14 is also Myth #5: Customer service is just plain common sense.

If good customer service came from having common sense, some of us would deliver it automatically and others of us would never be able to deliver it at all. Good customer service is an acquired skill. It takes training, focus, and role modeling. With a set of actions and attitudes, delivering good customer service can become more instinctive. Mary Jane reports, "The Borders on Michigan Avenue was, as can be expected, packed at the holidays. At least ten people were in each of the six register lines, so the wait was long. Then one of the baristas from the cafe came along with a tray and started passing out bites of an apple pastry and those little sample cups of hot cider with whipped cream and caramel. You can imagine that the entire atmosphere lightened after that. I don't know whose idea it was, but it was genius."

BAM! Blocker #15: The company has set a price point that doesn't leave enough margin to provide the level of service and/or quality that customers want.

Customer service takes financial investment. If there is not enough gross margin to add this type of overhead, the financial model for the company does not work. Certain aspects of customer service are going to be an ongoing challenge to every business, no matter what.

There are certain realities of serving customers that aren't pleasant and aren't going to change, but we can't be lulled into acceptance by **Myth #13: Customers can't expect a company to fix all complaints overnight. They need to have a little patience when something goes wrong.**

 Every company needs to be aware of each of these and devise solutions to address them. It doesn't do one bit of good to pretend that these things don't happen in your business. They do, probably right under your nose. It's better to acknowledge that these areas are going to be an ongoing problem and figure out how to deal with them.

Unpreventable challenges to customer service can occur when the business isn't prepared to counteract their effect

There are certain things that are beyond a company's control. Some of these things are going to disappoint and upset customers. No company, regardless of their competence, commitment, and the training, can completely eliminate all these things, so Be Prepared.

BAM! Blocker #16: It's inevitable that every business will keep customers waiting.

One thing in business is inevitable: wait time. You might not want it. You might hate it yourself, but there is no affordable way to ensure that customers will never have to wait.

From checkout lanes at grocery and big-box stores, to hold time for customer service and help lines, customer queuing is a problem for most businesses. We live in an ever-increasing fast-paced world. People don't like to wait—yet waiting is inevitable.

Therefore, every business has to figure out ways to prevent the wait or they'll contribute to customer dissatisfaction.

The first step is not to tell customers that they won't have to wait. The second step is to figure out how to make the customer wait without making them dissatisfied.

Think of all the ways your business makes customers wait:

- on telephone hold

- for a call-back

- in checkout lines

- to ask a floor salesperson a question

- in the waiting room

- to get on your calendar

From music while you are on hold to suggesting less busy times to shop or call, businesses try to come up with ways to make waiting more palatable. Many businesses try to entertain their customers while they wait to make it more bearable. Some ideas work and some of them don't. Microsoft used to have an "on hold" DJ playing music for customers. Many restaurants serve sample food in the waiting line. Disney entertains people in line.

Waiting in line is part of the customer's experience with you. Realize this and you have made a good start. The register lines at our local Costco store are notoriously long. The process moves as efficiently as possible. The computer systems are fast. The checkout people are well trained. The lanes are wide and well marked. But Costco does one more thing. On the wall that customers face when they are checking out, there is a large leader board that lists the top five checkers in terms of speed. It shows their photographs and the average number of customers they check out per hour. This public display tells customers that Costco is focused on checkout lines. It also tells a customer which checkout line is most likely to move you through the quickest, and it motivates checkers to move as quickly as possible. In the end, most of us will wait if someone acknowledges the waiting by saying, "I'll be right with you" or makes eye contact.

BAM! Blocker #17: Customers want a human relationship, and not every business can profitably provide that.

For them, dealing with a human is part of the "good" customer experience. For many companies, using computer technology—automated answering systems, Web-based information, or a kiosk—are necessary to hold down costs. As our survey suggested, people do like to do simple transactions with kiosks, but in the end, when there is a problem or a more complicated transaction, we want a human being there pronto. Your processes need to understand when technology can assist and when a human needs to get involved. As the MotiveQuest study cited, "personal" is the most important attribute. The key is how to deliver it with a combination of intelligent and intuitive technology and empathetic people who care about making their customers feel satisfied. Margie Heisler, an event-planning manager, told us that "The number one thing that would be considered good personal contact—to make it like you're talking to a real person, talking to a friend—I try to create a bond between myself and whoever I'm talking with to make it personal. I try to add a little humor."

JoAnne Pavin, owner of Soulutions to Health, believes that focus is critical. "I guess having undivided attention between you and your customer and making them feel like they're the most important part of the situation. And I guess the best thing I've learned is you fake it 'til you make it. Put a smile on your face until you get into a good mood. They're going to follow the energy you put out."

Tracey Welsh, general manager at Red Mountain Spa (which Barry has personally visited), tells us what the spirit of service means. "I tell employees to make a true connection with the guests. They want them to meet their goals—a relaxing vacation; weight loss; hike that last mountain—they are invested in seeing the guests get the value from experience. We follow that up at least four times per year; we have all-spa trainings, and those are focused on our standards of service: Gold Star—greet your guest, smile within ten feet; those ten points. Create those wonderful customer service moments without divulging all the steps it took to get there. You are blown away when someone uses your name in the public service industry—don't blow the illusion. How do I know your name? It pops up on the display… but don't be transparent."

Deborah House sums it up with something we can all relate to: "It is all about communication; just tell me why I'm waiting on this runway for an hour!"

BAM! Blocker #18: All businesses must use voice mail.

All businesses and virtually all individuals use some form of voice mail today (except Mary Jane's ninety-two year-old mother, who is completely independent yet absolutely refuses to leave a recorded message or use an answering machine). We have it on our cell phones and our home phones, and businesses can't live without it. The basic premise of voice mail is that a person is not going to be available one hundred percent of the time, and that leaving a specific message for that person will satisfy both parties more than not. However, this premise has been hijacked along the way. Using voice mail to avoid human contact is one of the biggest and most common barriers to building satisfied relationships with customers. It even has a name: *voice mail jail.* Answering the phone with a live person or setting the expectation on a returned call is critical.

BAM! Blocker #19: Well-trained and well-intended employees will not make mistakes that cause problems for customers.

Humans are human. We are all going to make mistakes. Customers are going to make mistakes, too. Identify mistakes and try to minimize their impact on the customer and company. Deborah House tells us, "I used to work at McDonald's, and we used to say, 'giving good customer service isn't giving away free hamburgers. It's about making people feel good about paying for your service.'"

BAM! Blocker #20: Employees may not be able to efficiently and cost-effectively address customer problems without degrading service in other areas.

One dissatisfied customer can take more of our time than a dozen who are satisfied. A business has to figure out how to effectively and affordably deal with these situations without making a dissatisfied customer more dissatisfied.

BAM! Blocker #21: Employees may not take the time to find out what the customers really think and feel.

There is no one bulletproof way to find out what's on customers' minds or in their guts. We give guidelines in Chapter 6 on what every company can do.

BAM! Blocker #22: Employees may not figure out the right balance of authority and employee empowerment.

Managers say they "empower" their employees, but most really just pay lip service to it. Be clear about what decisions employees should make and which ones need to be brought to management. Most customers hate front-line employees hiding behind management.

Tracey Welsh at Red Mountain Spa tells us, "People are afraid to make those decisions. It's a fear of retribution. It's one of the things my customer service manager talked about. If I give this guest something, I'm going to get in trouble. It's your responsibility to make the customer happy."

As customers, why do we put up with all this nonsense?

It makes you wonder what sort of implicit, unstated manifesto customers have unwillingly signed on to when they many times put up with so much nonsense to get their product or service. Have companies finally worn customers out? As customers, are we just too tired to fight anymore? We have frequently pondered these questions:

Q: Why do I wait all day for the cable person to come?

A: We have little choice on who we pick for cable, and the switching costs are high. We figure the other company is just as bad, and our service mostly works.

Q: Why do we wait in line at the post office for hours to get our passports?

A: We have no choice if we want to travel outside the country. We reason with ourselves we only have to renew it every ten years.

Q: Why do I wait in line at Starbucks for my double mocha latte for fifteen minutes?

A: We are addicted. There is something social in the experience. The place smells good. The line usually moves quickly. We expect to wait for a custom-made drink.

As a customer, why do you accept anything but *BAM!-good* customer service?

Wearily, most customer expectations are actually pretty low

In today's world, customer expectations are so low that anything a company does for customer service is more than customers expect. This is where the opportunity for the benefits of *BAM!-good* customer service lies.

A company can actually get a sustainable competitive advantage by offering great customer service. It makes you stand out from the crowd. As a small business consultant, Barry competes with thousands of other people with similar backgrounds and similar skills. One of the things that differentiates him from his competitors is that he will talk with a client anywhere and anytime. He commits to his clients that he will always return their call, e-mail, or text within sixty minutes.

When customers complain about customer service, do they really mean it?

Maybe customers aren't as upset as companies think they are. While there may be some chronic complainers out there, our experience is that when the customer finally complains, they are at a boiling point. It may not be this specific incident and could be built up over time with your company (and other companies). Unless the customer constantly calls into complain (which you should be tracking), take customer complaints seriously.

Maybe customers just are being pragmatic

They think that if they want lower prices, service is going to suffer. Up to a point, customers will put up with less customer service for a lower price. People camp out all night in the United States to get door busters the day after Thanksgiving, after a while, even Barry stopped shopping at Toys "R" Us because the service was so bad and he could never find anything. The low price did not compensate for the frustrating customer service experience of no one ever being there to help.

Depending on your business and the product or service you provide, your customers may put up with a lot of poor service. This is why so many customer service issues do not get addressed. For many companies, customers do not demand it and companies are permitted to "act badly" But at some point, if not corrected and customers actually have a meaningful choice, they will take their business someplace else if they can.

This chapter has covered the twenty-two roadblocks to delivering *BAM!-good* customer service, from beliefs, lamentations, and excuses, to preventable actions and attitudes, to unpreventable challenges like lines and e-mail that are simply going to be part of the deal.

Recognizing that all these conditions exist, we believe that to achieve *BAM!-good* customer service, companies need to strike a new agreement with their prospects and customers. It needs to be formal, public, and based on the honest intention and desire to help customers *feel* more satisfied—a manifesto to express their commitment to delivering *BAM!-good* customer service. Chapter 5 explains how to create such a two-way manifesto for your company and your customers.

Chapter 5:
The *BAM!-good* Customer Manifesto

Whenever you do business with your customer, there are spoken, unspoken, and written contracts. These agreements happen automatically as part of everyday normal transactions. Our lawyers insist that we write down the "important or high-value contracts." Much of the time, these contracts are not worth the paper they are written on because suing someone is typically a waste of money. What written contracts are good for is setting expectations between the parties involved.

When we sell something to someone or agree to buy something from someone, there is a basic, implied promise that the exchange will be done in a fair and mutually satisfying way. However, for *BAM!-good* customer service to take root, a business needs much more than good intentions, a fancy tagline, or even a promise.

The commitment you make to your customer needs to be a **manifesto**—a public declaration of all that you intend to do for the customer to make your business relationship mutually satisfying and keep them coming back.

With a public manifesto, customers will know exactly what they can expect from the company they are doing business with. Employees of the company also know exactly what they are committed to deliver to their customers. A manifesto holds the company to a standard without wiggle room. The customer manifesto is the most complete reflection of a company's attitude and actions in dealing with its customers.

Writing an effective customer manifesto

There is no such thing as a one-size-fits-all manifesto, but there are points that every company must make in their own way if a manifesto is to be effective, actionable, and believable. This is what delivering *BAM!-good* customer service is all about:

1. **We will deliver on what we promised.** Sounds simple, doesn't it? The company will deliver the product or service we promised at the price and method we agreed upon with the customer. But this can get tricky unless both the company and the customer are on the same page. Does the customer know exactly what they are buying? It is the company's obligation to make sure they do. Does the customer understand the ultimate or final price (now or over a period of time)? Are they receiving the service or product in the timeframe they agreed? Accomplishing this one time is easy. Doing it for every transaction for every customer becomes very difficult. This is what made McDonald's famous. No matter where you go in the country, the food will taste the same and get

delivered the same way. While you may not like McDonald's food, it consistently meets customers' expectations, and that is a big plus for their brand.

The goal of smaller companies is to achieve this level of consistency, no matter who or where the customer is, and no matter which employee is providing which product or service. The more complicated and diversified a company's products are, the more challenging delivering a consistent product or service becomes. A company may source raw materials, components, or even entire products from outside the company. Different employees may deliver the product or service in different ways depending on the industry or the geographic market they serve.

How is a company supposed to manage this ever-changing Rubik's Cube?

- **Create a standard to ensure that your company's version of "delivering on what we promised" means the identical thing to every employee.** It doesn't mean that the company will deliver what we promised when our suppliers deliver what they promised to us. It doesn't mean that we will deliver what we promised when we are having a good day. It doesn't mean that we will deliver when our revenues and margins are up. It is unconditional. It means we will deliver what we promised each time, every time. Period. This attitude must permeate the company culture with no exceptions.

- **Train everyone in the company on how to deliver on the standard.** For all employees, have a consistent training program and updates that teach everyone how to deliver the product or service in the consistent manner that the customers want and expect. Anticipate that there will be changes and modifications over time as customers and their needs and desires change.

- **Create a process to ensure that every product and service meets this standard.** This is important whether you source a finished good or materials that go into your or someone else's finished product. Have a process in place to audit the employees to ensure this is being done and to identify weaknesses in the process or people. When I ran my last computer mail-order company, we consistently monitored the call center to ensure employee process, performance, and customer satisfaction.

2. **If you are dissatisfied with our product or service, we will listen attentively to all your concerns.** As we have discussed before, listening and empathizing with the customer is really the first and most important step! Listening attentively (or whatever descriptor is fitting for your company to use) means listening with the intention of understanding the issue as completely as it takes to solve the customer's problem from their viewpoint and to help them feel satisfied.

3. **When things go wrong, we will be easy to reach in an economically feasible manner.** We will not lead you on a wild goose chase and put you through "voice mail jail" or a maze that would make any architect jealous. When you call any of our telephone numbers, you will always be able to talk to a real person by pressing zero. We *want* to be easy to reach

and will display our contact information clearly on our Web site. We will provide multiple ways to contact us, including telephone, e-mail, and online chat.

This is of critical importance. As we discussed earlier, the main objective that a dissatisfied customer has is first to be listened to and empathized with. By being easy to reach, you accomplish your first objective and put the customer in a frame of mind that gives you the best chance to solve their concern at the lowest cost and with the least disruption.

4. **We will resolve your issues in a reasonable manner and in a reasonable time frame, give you a refund, or compensate you in a manner that leaves you as satisfied as possible.** This links back to Myth #1 (No customer is always right) and Myth #2 (No customer is always wrong to the value of a customer. The company gets to create the definition for "reasonable manner" and "reasonable time frame." These must be definitions that the customers agree with and are economically profitable for the company. In a world that is moving faster and faster, where buyers seem to have less and less patience, the time frame becomes critical. What the company provides to the customer also influences expectations. If you are delivering auto towing service or pepperoni pizza, you need to respond more quickly than if you are delivering for the United States Postal Service.

Unless you have caused collateral damage in providing your service or product, a full refund delivered quickly and graciously will usually satisfy the customer. Sometimes it is better to issue a refund and make the problem go away than to invest the time of more people trying to solve the issue a different way.

This is a quick cost-and-benefit analysis that every employee needs to be trained to do. For example, when you want to return low-priced products to Oriental Trading Company, they tell you not to send them back. Instead, they give you a refund and ask you to donate the products to charity. Their goods are priced inexpensively, so the cost of processing a return doesn't make sense. Think about the impression you can make on the customer for doing this! A refund also releases you from the implied contract with the customer. This is a good thing, because sometimes you do not want to have that dissatisfied customer as a customer. Some customers are unable to be satisfied. By giving a refund, at the very least you end your obligations to them (or so you hope).

5. **We will admit when we made a mistake.** The best chance to resolve a customer concern is to admit that a mistake was made by your company. Teach your employees to take personal responsibility and not pass either the blame or resolution to fix to someone else or another department in the company. It is quite the disturbing trend in business when the person who is there to solve your concern passes the blame on to another part of the company or back to the customer. It is important to remember that in the eyes of the customer, you are all one company, and saying that it is another department's fault can cause the customer to feel more dissatisfied about the company. Of course, this means that the company must be willing to not beat its employees up for every mistake. When an employee takes responsibility for a customer, he or she is not held to be personally at fault.

The Chicago Transit Authority (CTA) has a terrific online service that allows riders to check the arrival times of buses from their iPhone, Blackberry, or computer. Barry boarded a bus and told the driver that its GPS device was probably out since he could not track the bus coming from his iPhone. The driver said, "Call the office; I have nothing to do with this." What the driver could have said was, "Thank you for telling me. I can't place a call while I'm driving (it's illegal in Chicago). Would you please call this number to report the problem?" Of course, this would mean that the CTA actually wants to learn about these problems, has set up a number to receive the reports, and has trained each and every bus driver on what to say to riders when this occurs.

6. **We will empower our employees to solve your issue at the point it occurs.** All our employees will be able to help you, and you will not have to wait for "the manager." We want to resolve the issue as soon as possible. The customer does not always want to wait for a "supervisor" or have some nameless and faceless person make a decision about them.

   Training inside of your company must be such that the people on the front lines can actually help the customer with specific actions. This takes hiring people who are not afraid to act on their own within the guidelines that the company sets. It takes clear objectives through training of these employees. Most importantly, it takes trusting your employees to take the appropriate action and then getting out of the way so they can do it. This goes back to the beginning of hiring the right people. Monitoring what they are doing in specific situations will help. You also need to train the supervisor to coach the employees on what they can and cannot do on their own.

The best time to reinforce this is when the employee brings an issue to the supervisor that can be solved by the employee on their own.

7. **We will not force you to buy something you do not want.** Do not put undue restrictions on what your customers can buy by over-bundling. Bundling of products may offer additional value, but a customer should not be required to get the one thing they really want through buying a bunch of things they don't want. Cable companies are notorious for this. To get the best price from the cable company, consumers frequently need to buy all Internet, cable, and phone service in a bundle. This makes people get all kinds of channels that they don't want, which they have to scan through to find the few programs they really do want to watch.

   During the Swine Flu (H1N1) scare of 2009, Lysol made a portable hand sanitizer that was in high demand and short supply. However, the only way we saw this sold at the retail store was bundled with a large can or their regular spray product. This isn't good marketing; it's customer annoyance.

8. **We will make it easy to end our business relationship.** Of course we want to keep you as a customer, but we understand that our products and services are not for everyone. We will make it easy to stop being your provider in a courteous and quick manner, and be hopeful that you will return one day. We will wish you well, conclude any unfinished business, release you from any obligations we feel you have to us, do our best to satisfy any obligations you feel we have to you, and then move on.

   It is typically so easy to sign up to start doing business with a company. Sometimes, it can be a nightmare when you want to stop. Have you ever tried to find how to cancel an online service? You know that the right button must be hidden in there somewhere, yet it turns into a treasure hunt. It is even more maddening is when you want to cancel your account to get passed to a "special team" that handles these kinds of things. This feels like punishment, being manipulated into attending a timeshare lecture, or being forced to go to traffic school. Thou shalt not punish the customer. Customers come and go—deal with it.

Last year, Barry tried to quit an electronic fax service because he found a cheaper one. He contacted their customer service after searching on the site. He had the darnedest time trying to cancel the service. The texting went like this:

Eric J: Hello, Barry. Welcome to j2 Global online support. I am Eric, your online live support representative. How are you doing today?

Barry M: I want to cancel my account. I found a cheaper alternative in Trustfax.com at $4.95 a month. How do I cancel?

Eric J: I'm sorry to hear that you wish to leave our services. Could you please provide me with your fax number associated with your account for verification?

Barry M: 773.333.1234

Eric J: Thank you for providing your information. Please give me a moment while I go through your records. Barry, in the current situation, we will waive the monthly fee for two months. This way you will be able to keep your account, which will enable you to send and receive faxes. You will also be able to use all of our services and re-evaluate it for your faxing needs. During this period, you will not be charged any monthly fee. We are suggesting this so that you can give it a second thought, as you will not be paying $16.95 for the next two billing cycles. Your eFax account will be credited with $33.90 so that you may utilize our services without being billed our monthly fee for the next two billing cycles. Since you will not be charged any monthly fee for the next two months, you could keep the number 'til then. If you find that you need our services during this period, then you will still have the account. If, however, you still feel that you do not have any use for our services by the end of this two-month credit period, then you can always contact us anytime. Would you like that?

Barry M: No, please just cancel the account. Sorry and thank you.

Eric J: Barry, I completely understand your wish to discontinue. Since you have already paid for the month, we do not want you to lose out on the money. I suggest that you retain this number at least 'til the end of the two-month credit offer, as you will not be charged any monthly fee for the two months.

Barry M: Here is the problem: I will forget in two months to cancel it.

Eric J: As a goodwill gesture to continue our association, we will offer you an additional gift balance of $10 along with the monthly credit, which will enable you to send up to 100 additional fax pages free of cost (per page per minute within the U.S. and Canada). During this two-month credit period, you can keep this service active, and if you use it once in these two months, we will be more than happy that we were able to serve you. If you do not wish to continue beyond this waiver period, then there is no obligation to continue. There are no contracts. All you would need to do is contact us just once, anytime during this credit period to re-confirm your decision. We are at your service, round the clock, twenty-four hours a day, seven days a week.

Barry M: Please just cancel it. This should not be hard. I have used your service for years and now I want to discontinue it.

Provide excellent service on the way in and out. You never know when they will be back. I recently canceled my service for PR Leads. Dan Janal, the owner, sent me a very different e-mail. He asked me why I was leaving and if he could do anything for me to provide better service. He welcomed me to come back anytime. It may surprise you that a customer can still give your business a good reference because the way you handled them coming and leaving.

9. **We will not charge separate nuisance fees or surcharges.** There is nothing more maddening than buying products for one price and being charged all sorts of unexpected nuisance fees. We have all been in restaurants where they charge for splitting an entrée or have minimum amounts per person. This is nonsense and completely at odds with offering *BAM!-good* customer service the way the customer wants it. The absolute worst in our opinion are the de-registration and re-registration charges that cellular carriers tack on when a subscriber buys a new telephone. These charges are assessed

even when a person is replacing a phone that breaks. It would seem that cellular carriers who receive their revenue from monthly service charges would want to make it as inexpensive and easy as possible for subscribers to be up and on the network.

Mail-order companies were famous for "handling charges," and we have recently seen "fuel surcharges" on our bills with the rapid change in energy prices. Customers can see through this as a way to make extra money or defray costs. This breaks the manifesto. Companies easily add on these surcharges, but most of the time they become permanent. Interestingly, many of the most successful Internet companies do not charge handling or even shipping charges.

Barry was in Australia going to a cruise to the Great Barrier Reef. His group was picked up at the hotel by a bus from the cruise company. They had prepaid for the trip months earlier and traveled over an hour to get to the location where the cruise began. When they arrived, they were informed that there would be a fuel surcharge of $10 per person if they wanted to go on the cruise. What? They had paid hundreds of dollars ahead of time, traveled an hour by bus, and now the cruise operator was telling the group that if they wanted to get on the boat, it was going to cost more money! This is holding customers hostage! Foul.

A limo service in Chicago, Smart Car, implemented a "fuel surcharge" when gasoline was $4.50 a gallon. When gas the next month went down to $2.00 a gallon, they still did not remove the fuel surcharge. We did not understand this. When questioned, they eventually changed the name to something else. They should just have called it "price increase." *BAM!*

Although they provide excellent service, we stopped using them.

As a company, take the risk that your costs will go up or down. If your prices went down, would you charge less? Unlikely. You would take the lower costs as added profit. When costs go up, you bear the risk. You can raise overall prices, but then customers can choose to find a less expensive company to do business with. Last-minute price increases break the manifesto. If your costs go up so much you have to increase prices, then increase prices. Tacking on surcharges not only looks like bad business—it is.

10. **We will treat you with respect and dignity at all times.** This means that we will listen attentively when you talk and not interrupt you. We will try to see your point of view. We will speak in a calm tone of voice without expressions of frustration or disgust. We will not say one thing to your face and another when we hang up the phone. We will tell you when we disagree and why, but our goal is to express our opinion and also see your point of view.

Dealing with customers can be frustrating. We all get angry, but our job is to be just as effective with customers at the beginning of the day as the end of the day. Many days this is a challenge. Front-line employees need to have ways to release their frustration and enough breaks in their routine so their approach remains effective.

The idea of a having a small room where any employee can scream or yell to let go of frustrations about customers isn't that far off base. In any event, welcome all kinds of feedback from your staff. Try to vary their activities so they can talk to satisfied and dissatisfied customers. It is especially difficult to handle all problems all day long.

11. **When we decide to change something in our agreement (raise or lower our prices, alter our hours, drop or add a service or product), we will tell you in advance in a very public way.** In a business relationship, things change. When they do, we will communicate fully in enough time so that you can make the choices you need to make. There is nothing inherently wrong with raising prices. If you add value to your customers, they will accept this as a part of doing business. If you need to alter your terms of service or drop an unprofitable product, your customers may not be happy, but they will understand. Most people are not unreasonable. The key is to give customers advance notice so they can make the decision they need to make based on what the company plans to do. Unfortunately, too many companies try to push through stealth price increases, hoping that their customers won't notice.

In 2009, Facebook covertly changed their terms of service in a way that affected the ownership of material users placed on their site. When it finally was exposed, the blogosphere went crazy and Facebook had to rescind the policy. If they had been forthcoming with their change, customers might have accepted it. Unless it's your birthday, no one likes surprises—that especially includes your customers.

12. **We will never, ever, ever give or sell any information about you without your permission.** This is probably the biggest contribution that the Internet has made in the age of customer service. Personal information is easily accessible in mass quantities from many databases. Companies must never ever share this information with anyone outside the company

without customers' explicit permission. We recommend devoting a visible area of the company's Web site to clearly and publicly state how customer information is used inside the company, under what conditions the company would ever share it, and an easy-to-use step for customers to opt out.

13. **We will not fill your e-mail or your mailbox with marketing material you don't want to see.** We will make it easy for you to opt in or out of information that we send. Use a strict opt-in service with an online marketing system (for example, Constant Contact, Vertical Response, or Exact Target) that allows users at any time to opt out of getting your information, and you are unable to send it to them. These systems respect customers' privacy and help you and your company conform to spamming laws and regulations.

14. **We will offer you several convenient ways to provide feedback on our products and services.** If you share your opinions and experiences with us, we will listen to what you have to say. You will know that we listened because we will respond to you and follow up in a reasonable time frame. It is important to understand that customers may want to give the company feedback in many different forms at many different points of the sales, delivery, and service process. The company wants to be able to ask for and accept feedback from customers at all these stages. Show that you listen by responding immediately through automatic computer means, and then set the expectation on when and how a real person will address their concern and respond.

15. **In every situation, we will ask you what it would take to make you feel satisfied.** As business people, most of us are not mind readers. We can't begin to guess what will really

make our customer feel happy or satisfied since, as we have discussed, this feeling varies from customer to customer and time to time. If we ask the customer the specific question, "What will it take to make you feel satisfied?" and we are able to do that as a company economically, then we can shorten the service cycle and greatly increase our odds of delivering *BAM!-good* customer service and creating a happy and satisfied customer.

What your customer manifesto should *not* include

A customer manifesto is a living document, but it shouldn't be a document that changes all the time. The goal is to provide a framework of doing business that is broad enough to contain the whole relationship but specific enough to clearly spell out the company's intent when it comes to dealing with customers. This does not include **Myth # 18: Companies achieve customer service by under-promising and over-delivering.**

The goal is to provide a framework of doing business that is broad enough to contain the whole relationship but specific enough to clearly spell out the company's intent when it comes to dealing with customers.

1. **Under-promise and over-deliver.** This concept is ridiculous because it will result in not attracting the customers we are targeting because they will think that we are unable to meet their needs. We need to map out exactly what we will do for

customers and tell them that. It is also economically difficult because many clients will not pay for excessive quality. If your company offers a baker's dozen (thirteen bagels instead of twelve), should it give fifteen bagels so the customer is even more satisfied? Try this at Einstein's Bagels and see what looks you get before they say no. By setting expectations at the right level, a company can still provide products and services that produce very satisfied customers. In fact, in this age of disappointments and deteriorating service, doing business with a company that is consistent and does exactly what it says is a highly desirable and refreshing change.

2. **Make commitments that are not economically reasonable to keep.** Provide excellent customer service because it makes economic sense for business. (Re-read Chapter 3.) Don't provide a level of service that will make your company unprofitable. A company especially needs to pay attention to their return policy and the promise on how quickly they will react to a concern. We always wondered how specialty retailer Hammacher Schlemmer can have a lifetime guarantee on all the products they sell. According to their return policy, they will accept their products back at any time. We have tested their return policy many times, even returning something after ten years! Under this policy, it always seems we are only "renting" things from them since we can always return them! It amazes us how few things we actually do return.

   Your return policy needs to be economically feasible. If you have a thirty-day return policy, you will need to carry the liabilities for this on your balance sheet. If your return policy is six months, the liability grows. Within this limit, you also need to be flexible if the return comes on the thirty-first or sixty-first day.

3. **Make promises that the company doesn't intend to keep.** If you promise to get back to someone within an hour, ensure you have the staff to do that. If you promise that hold times will be less than five minutes, staff for that. Customers don't forget the little things. Broken promises breed customer dissatisfaction and undermine your entire manifesto. There is no room for winks or platitudes in a manifesto, no matter how tempting this may be. Only state what you can actually do and economically sustain. It is better not to make a promise than to make one and break it.

4. **Make specific promises, whether you can keep them or not.** A manifesto is a reflection of attitude and intent. Save the specifics for the action plan. It will also give you room for individual interpretation by employees and the flexibility to change over time as customer and business needs change.

How to develop a manifesto?

You can copy what we wrote here, (see the Appendices for easy scanning) or you can customize your own. To customize your own, answer the following questions.

1. **If I were selling to myself, what would I want?** Rank your answers based on impact, cost, and practicality.

2. **What do I like that other businesses offer me as their customer?** No need here to recreate the wheel. What do other companies do especially well that you like? One of our customer service idols has always been Shelly Malkin at Perl Mortgage. She always returns e-mails and calls seemingly

instantaneously. When we try to provide great service we think, "What would Shelly do?"

3. **What do I hate that other businesses offer me as their customer?** Who are the customer service villains on your list? What is it that they do that you especially hate? Ensure that you do not do those things.

4. **What is economically feasible for my company to offer?** Be realistic with your business model. What kind of return policy can you afford? What type of staff can you have in the store to service customers? How many people can you have on the phone at one time? As mentioned, years ago, Microsoft's hold times for customer service were so long that they hired a DJ for their music on hold! We imagine this was an economical solution—entertain the people on hold instead of offering shorter hold times.

5. **What is economically not feasible for me to provide that I might be tempted to provide?** Ensure that your company can provide whatever you promise in good and bad economic times. Don't let grandiose plans or ego lead your company off the track of what is practical for your business.

6. **What do my customers expect?** Be a mystery shopper of your own company. Buy from it anonymously to find out exactly what your customers are experiencing.

7. **What do your employees think should be in your manifesto?** Ask them, is this what customers want? Can we keep these promises to them?

Under what conditions should a manifesto change?

The goal is to keep your word, but as with any agreement, external conditions can change. When changes are frequent or significant enough, sit down and talk with your customers first. But sometimes changing the manifesto is the only option.

1. **The customer has broken the contract (sometimes even more than once).** Foul ball! You were scheduled to install that big-screen TV at 3:00 p.m. today and no one was home. You skipped your private Pilates training session because you were running late and never called the studio. Unless this was a misunderstanding, then the customer is responsible for missed appointments. We don't object to the companies that we do business with charging us for missed appointments. It's nice when they waive this for us when we have a true emergency, but if they don't we understand and even appreciate their clear statement of these policies.

2. **The customer is being totally unreasonable by all business standards.** The customer attitude is disproportional to the issue at hand. They are verbally abusing your staff. The economic reimbursement that they hope for is totally unreasonable given the transaction. In this case, do the best you can, give a refund, and move on.

3. **You have already "fired" the customer, but they keep calling or contacting you anyway.**
   Report them or block them. This falls under the category of vengeance or punitive actions by the customer. It is abusive and stressful to your employees. It will interfere with the service of other customers who are profitable for you.

4. **The business has changed. The competition, marketplace, or economy has changed.** Maybe you are going through tough times. Maybe you lost a lease. Maybe something you have been doing in the past can't be done anymore. Maybe the cost of your raw materials has spiked through the roof. Maybe you simply want to do business differently. Maybe there is some new technology that makes something possible that wasn't possible before. It's okay. What's not okay is to delay telling the customers so they can then decide how they want to react.

The customer should have a manifesto, too.

The manifesto is a two-way street. Not that bad customer service is the customer's fault, but they do have a part in improving it. Ask your customers if they would be willing to join you in the manifesto process. Start by inviting the customers you really care about to have a manifesto discussion with you. As a starting point, offer a draft of a customer manifesto that includes:

1. **I will always notify the company when I am dissatisfied with their product or service. I will not suffer in silence or complain to others before I complain to the company.** This is the big one. If we as business people could only guarantee one thing from our customers, this would be the one we would want. So many customers go away disgruntled, and the company never finds out. For companies choosing to deliver *BAM!-good* customer service, finding a way to guarantee that our customers tell us when they are dissatisfied is a huge game changer. A way to start is to have mechanisms and

feedback loops that everyone understands and that work to make it easy to catch a complaint and contact the company.

Customers, complain when you are dissatisfied. You are doing the company a service; if you are dissatisfied, there are probably others who are as well, but do not bring it up to the company. Remember that complaints can be voiced in a respectful and productive way.

2. **I will state my problem as clearly and concisely as possible.** This again is a difficult one. Dissatisfied customers come to the table with so much anger and baggage that it is sometimes hard to get to the root of the problem. Companies can help remedy this situation by asking a concise questions that get at the real issue and keep out the emotion. The dissatisfied customer can come to the call with a concise set of notes and chronology of events.

3. **I will do whatever I can to not blame the person who answered the phone and try to keep my personal anger out of the conversation.** As previously stated, customer service reps need to be trained in listening and empathy skills. This is above all what the customer really wants. I will do my best to not personally blame or yell at the person answering the phone. They are trying to help me. I will not swear or be verbally abusive.

4. **I will save documentation on the specific issue and all my receipts.** Companies are not mind readers and they are unable to keep track of everything in their database. Keep your receipts, letters, and e-mails that closely track the issue you are trying to solve. This will make it easy for the company to justify an action that satisfies you.

5. **I will be prepared to tell the company what I would like to remedy the situation in reasonable economic terms.** Many times a company does not really know what it will take to satisfy your concern. Be prepared with a reasonable suggestion. A business needs to make a profit. Because your newspaper did not get delivered today does not mean you should now get a free subscription to the paper for the year.

6. **I won't be a pest.** Getting the company to provide good customer service is not a sport. Many times, the best course of action is to get a refund and find another company that can meet your expectations.

What are the steps that you actually can take to deliver *BAM!-good* customer service in a self-service world? Turn the page for Chapter 6.

Chapter 6:
How to Deliver
BAM!-good Customer Service
in a Self-Service World

The first consideration in delivering *BAM!-good* customer service is to understand what your customers think about the service your company is (or is not) delivering today. No matter how well or poorly a company treats its customers, most businesses yearn for feedback from customers. The challenge is how to get information from customers that is a true reflection of how they feel and that the company can take action on.

Feedback usually only happens under two circumstances. One, the company tends to ask for feedback right after the initial transaction and then not much after that. And, two, many customers will initiate feedback only when there is a problem and they are fairly fed up. Manish Patel, CEO of Where 2 Get It, has learned from this. "If we're only speaking to the customer every time their bill is due, they think all we care about is money. It's a constant dialogue between the corporation and the customer that builds an ongoing relationship." When we sit in first class and the flight attendant introduces himself and calls us by our first name that forms a relationship.

Make it easy and convenient to offer feedback at every interaction a customer has with your company. Each customer is a unique human with interests, needs, and desires that vary constantly; your customers will want to give feedback at many different intersections in your relationship and in different ways that will be different at different times. One size does not fit all—not even for one given customer. This means that the company, who wants to use customer feedback as an input to delivering *BAM!-good* customer service, must provide its customers the opportunity to give feedback in person, over the phone, via voice mail, over the Internet, or by written letter. If a company asks and makes it easy for customers to respond from all these methods, more varied customers will respond.

What methods should a company use? That depends on the company's target customers and which method they would most likely use, but before a company can settle on the appropriate methods, it is important to understand the limits of measuring anything. It is always a challenge of putting non-quantifiable things into mathematical terms. What could be more qualitative than a customer's feeling of satisfaction? Yet this is what we have to do to create a measure of customer service that a company can use to adapt its attitude and actions to move toward *BAM!-good* customer service. While anecdotal feedback is fine, the manager always looks for numbers.

Direct methods

- *Ask and you might receive.* But receive what? It all depends on how, who, and when you ask. There are plenty of consultants and other experts who can and will for a fee design and conduct a survey to get the exact type of feedback you say you are looking for, but that's not the point. A company needs to get feedback that will help improve the connection with its customers and ultimately build a more profitable business. And that might not be what the company is asking for. *Yes, survey your customers, but when?* Many connection points are possible.

- *At the time of the point-of-sale transaction for a product*: This can be an extremely inaccurate way to get an idea of what your customers think. Primarily, this is likely the time the customer is the most satisfied since so much of the company's resources are usually focused here. We see these surveys hastily taped to receipts and promising discounts on your next visit if you fill them out. Sometimes they also have a special note that reads:

  "If you can't give us the highest rating right now, call the manager at ...." Talk about "priming the pump." This is an effort, often by the local staff, to skew the evaluations to their benefit, most likely because some well-intended manager or consultant suggested that the company evaluate or reward employees based on customer feedback to these surveys.

  This virtually ensures that the company won't receive the type of feedback it needs to improve customer satisfaction. Many customers will not fill out the survey for a simple transaction since they are ready to leave after completing their transaction. Those who do fill out the survey at this point typically are biased toward the positive on the product or overly influenced by the sales staff seeking a positive outcome.

In principle, there is nothing wrong with offering incentives to fill out a survey. We suggest that instead of offering a discount toward future purchases, the company offer the incentive as a donation to a third party. David Rabjohns, CEO at MotiveQuest, offers a $50 donation on behalf of his customers to the Darfur Relief Fund. As David writes in his e-mail, "So please find five minutes to fill out the survey, which will actually take you less time than finding the address of a charity and sending a check, and help this little girl and her friends."

- *Directly after completion of the job or stay*: Many times these evaluations are rushed at checkout for a service or at the end of a consulting assignment. If your company does this, evaluations should be presented in a consistent manner, and the customer should have the ability to complete it later and conveniently send it in to the company. These types of surveys need to be aggregated over a long period of time to get a true actionable trend.

- *Surveys sent as a post-sale follow-on*: We always liked the timing of this. Although the chances of getting the survey completed are lower, a follow-on survey does two additional things: It can thank the customer again for their purchase, and it puts the company name and logo forward to remind customers to use you again. If you made a lasting impression (positive or negative), you will get more balanced feedback. An Internet tool called Survey Monkey is an easy way to survey your customers and analyze them.

What do you measure?

Only ask questions that are truly actionable. For example, if you ask, "Did you like us?" what can you do as a result of the answer you get? This is a useless question because, although it may make you feel good or bad, there is not a specific action you can take with the results. Be specific in your questions so they can lead you to take specific actions. For example, ask, "Did you receive a call-back after your initial order?" The answer to this question will let you know if the staff is following the procedures. If they are not, you can change the process or training of your staff to accomplish the desired goal.

One of the most popular questions to ask comes from Fred Reichheld and his Net Promoter team, who made the phrase "Would you recommend us to a colleague or friend" the way to measure the ultimate level of satisfaction.[10]

Here are questions we suggest you ask:

1. **Do you plan to use our services or buy our product in the future?** If customers say they will buy again from you, this suggests a certain level of satisfaction. While this does not guarantee the highest level of satisfaction, typically, one's loyalty runs so high that they will continue to buy if they are really angry. This question tends to get answered by happy, angry, and even neutral customers.

2. **Is there anyone at the company who did a particularly great job or a poor one?** Many customers connect or focus on an individual who provided the service or interacted with them in the transaction. This may be positive or negative, but many customers have an easy time associating that satisfaction with a person rather than the company as a whole. This question tends to get answered more fully by the very happy or very angry since someone made a very strong impression.

3. **Why did you choose to do business with us?** This question always gets at the referral source and can identify what part of your marketing mix is working more effectively for the customers who answer the question. For the best calculation, offer this as a multiple-choice answer with a follow-up to identify a specific source. Answers to this question, if they are specific, help the company identify why customers buy, and if matched to some demographic analysis, can provide information to help the company duplicate its success with more customers who, at least to some degree, match the demographics of existing, satisfied customers.

4. **Can you tell us of friends or associates who may be interested in using our service?** This is similar to Fred Reichheld's Net Promoter question, but with two important distinctions. First, if the customer is willing to give a referral, this means they feel satisfied. They will not put their reputation on the line unless they like what they have seen and experienced at your company. Secondly, the referral is a well-qualified lead that you can turn into a prospect. When a company gets a lead from a trusted referral, it is an opportunity to leapfrog you ahead of all the other people the lead is considering buying from.

For example, MotiveQuest uses a survey for all of their client engagements.[11]

They ask about quality of:

- The initial proposal

- The research

- The discussion around objectives

- The initial data report

- The interim discussion

- The final verbal debrief

- The insights

- The final report

By breaking the feedback for their service into each of its parts, they give the client the opportunity to comment on each phase of interaction with them, and as a result focus on the segments of their process that need to be improved. MotiveQuest is then brave enough to ask, "Did our research, insights, and recommendations impart your actions or decisions?" They are asking, did you use what we told you? They then ask, "What would you like us to do differently if we work together again?" Get ready for the answer.

How do you survey for satisfaction if you are a monopoly?

As the police officer mentioned in Chapter 3 wrote, "How do we measure satisfaction when we are necessary and customers have no free-market choice and poor performance (crime rates going up) leads to increased demands for service?" In other words, getting customer feedback if you are a monopoly may not matter much. Intuitively, this makes sense, and is one of the reasons that none of us like monopolies and few of us can point to one that offers *BAM!-good* customer service. By their very existence, they don't have to care about how their customers feel—at least until another choice comes along. Our message to monopolies is this: don't waste resources on a system of customer feedback. Why? First, let's go back to the reason to provide *BAM!-good* customer service: to increase revenue by retaining existing and attracting new customers. With a true monopoly, there is no measurable economic motivation in this regard. The people who need what the monopoly provides (for example, electricity) will buy from the monopoly because they have no other source. The people who don't need what the monopoly provides won't buy from it no matter what.

Second, even if ethics, pride, or altruism could possibly be a motivator for the monopoly, (highly doubtful, as most monopolies are motivated mainly by remaining a monopoly), as discussed in Chapter 3, these are not the basis for *BAM!-good* customer service.

Finally, by asking for customer input, the monopoly will create unnecessary work for itself and unrealistic expectations for its customers since it is highly unlikely that a monopoly will act on any information it receives in surveys. Monopolies should only ask for feedback from their customers if part of the monopoly's business is clearly broken, or if they are looking to placate consumers or regulatory bodies by creating a little good public relations.

Mystery shopping: another direct measure of the customer.

This has always been our dream job—to get paid for shopping. The billion-dollar secret shopper industry is a tool used by marketing research companies to measure the quality of retail service and to gather specific information about products or services. The mystery shopper anonymously shops the product, asks questions, or behaves in a specific way. They then give a detailed report to the company.

Some items that typically get recorded:

- How long it takes before the mystery shopper is greeted or what their initial shopping experience is like

- The name of the employee who helped them

- The employee's attitude

- The types of products offered

- If the employee asked for the sale

- Compliance with company standards such as service, appearance, and presentation

Online and other social media receive and measure customer service

Without asking the customer directly, what other tools are there to collect the customer satisfaction data we want? It is becoming an increasingly transparent world with the Internet and the blogosphere. Every consumer is a critic and a writer. Customers give feedback and comment on your business whether you ask or not. Every company needs to be aware that these virtual conversations are happening and needs to find out what is being said.

A caution: resist the temptation to shape these conversations; this can backfire on you, and Internet communities have very long memories. David Rabjohns at MotiveQuest says, "The key is to treat everybody with respect. For example, when Toyota wanted to reach out to some of their most influential Prius mavens, they started by contacting the moderators of the Prius forum, not the mavens themselves. It is important that companies work with experts who are sensitive to the field, follow the ethical guidelines, and avoid blundering in like a wedding crasher with a case of beer shouting 'yeah!'"

Utilizing online and social media tools has taken on an increased importance. According to Terry St. Marie, Senior VP of Bresnan Communications, before companies can successfully incorporate these tools into their customer service strategy, we have to ensure we are doing "…the analog stuff right. If you don't do the face-to-face, person-to-person things right, then you will use social media methods just to put out fires started by your shortfalls in these other areas. Every company first needs to build a call center that is responsive and trained to treat the customer with respect. If we don't do this well, customers will use social media to lash out at the company in a public way."

Some companies have used Internet technology to get more impersonal with the customer as only a convenience for the company. Scott Jordan, CEO at SCOTTEVEST, states that "there used to be a time when by using technology, companies wanted to seem big. Now using technology, companies want to seem small and personal to their customer." Other companies seem oblivious. When Barry recently bought a refrigerator from Sears, he was greeted the next day with a "robocall" asking to him complete a survey by telephone. He hung up.

Live streaming video or online chat

Companies are now using live streaming video to get closer to their customers. SCOTTEVEST may be the only company to use a live video streaming application called Stickam so customers can watch what is going on at the office, at the store, and in the warehouse. Owner Scott Jordan believes this provides trust and transparency to his customers because they can see what is going on at his company. Scott also regularly interacts with customers through video e-mail, live chat, and Twitter.

Twitter and Facebook

If your company has a customer profile set up—and if you don't, you should—your customers will be talking about you on Twitter and Facebook. Some companies monitor these sites (personally and through automated tools) so they can respond to what is said about them. Marshall Makstein of eSlide once complained on Twitter about one of his vendors—to his surprise and delight, he received an e-mail from them within an hour. Other companies set up communities on these sites for their customers to share and talk to each other. This is a convenience for the customers and builds community for the company, but more importantly, it solicits feedback companies can use.

Web tools

Social media on the Internet has become so popular that we actually put more trust in what peers, bloggers, and other Internet users say about a company than any other type of advertisement or paid endorsement.

Amazon's and eBay's systems were revolutionary when they first came out. When eBay began, buyers and sellers rated each other; eBay kept score. After many complaints from sellers, eBay has halted the seller rating system—a step that we don't agree with. To us, this is an important metric and goes a long way in providing the confidence that we need to do business with a stranger. The trustworthy rating of both buyer and seller on eBay did influence our selling *and* buying decisions. For us, it was a real-life example of a manifesto between buyer and seller.

On Amazon, we always check out the reviews of the products to see what users have to say. Sometimes people even post videos. User comments are viewed by shoppers and buyers as much more unbiased than professional reviewers in newspapers and magazine are.

The origin of the eBay rating system comes from the ideas of building a trustworthy environment where both buyers and sellers are able to exchange products through Internet commerce. Pierre Omidyar, founder of eBay, devoted his time to developing a system to make it easier for strangers to conduct business over the Internet.

According to Omidyar, "Most people are honest. And they mean well. Some people go out of their way to make things right. Pierre put his hope in each registered member. Their participation would result in driving dishonest users away from the auction community. This is not to say that there aren't any users who are deceiving; it is simply a fact of life. The user feedback form was created for the notion of giving praise where it is due, and to make complaints where appropriate. The creation of this social community is the driving force behind eBay's success."[12]

Similar to the original eBay, Amazon also developed a rating system in which registered users can leave both negative and positive feedback. Amazon and eBay incorporate feedback forums into their customer service strategy and review comments made on a regular basis. Further, Amazon has incorporated its user rating system into a sales strategy by recommending other products based on what other users purchased. Based on Amazon's rating system, the Web-based retailer has developed its service offerings from just selling books, to merchandising over the Internet an array of products ranging from home appliances to music.

Web sites

Yelp (www.yelp.com) is a directory of reviews of local retail businesses. A typical generic search (i.e., kosher food) includes a list pertaining to the user's search, providing a map and directions (using Google Maps), a five-star rating system, a users' reviews, and business details including business address, operating hours, pricing, accessibility, and parking. Yelp also makes it possible for business owners to upload their own information or edit already existing information.

The Web site combines both local reviews and social networking functionality to create a local online community. Similar to Amazon and eBay, user reviews create an open reputation system. Site visitors see which users are the most popular, respected, and productive; how long each has been a member; and which have interests similar to theirs.

The company strengthens its online community through offline events. These events take place at nightclubs, bars, restaurants, and cultural venues in various cities across the United States. Yelp then provides an "elite" tag for loyal contributors to the site. These members receive a special indicator on their personalized page for every year they author a specific number of reviews. This concept is meant to indicate that the user is a trusted source for reviews and feedback. As with many review sites, Yelp has been criticized over the fairness of negative reviews. Some business owners have even posted "No Yelpers" signs in frustration on their Web site and even at storefronts. Under its terms and conditions, Yelp states that it will not censor user comments, although it does remove favorable and unfavorable reviews that are considered "suspicious."

Getsatisfaction (getsatisfaction.com) acts as a tool to connect and engage customers with companies. The process is based on a few offered guidelines for both customers and companies in an easy-to-use interface. Customers of a product or company can ask questions, make suggestions, report problems, or post testimonials. Employees of the company can reply to them in the public space, and other users/customers of the company can respond. Getsatisfaction is a community that helps people get the most from the products they use, and where companies are encouraged to get "real" with their customers. So far, there are 7,000 registered companies; more than half of them are involving current employees in what Getsatisfaction.com calls "outcome-oriented discussion." Everyone is invited to post questions, answers, or concerns, or simply to post anything they have to say.

As a user of the site, you are free to ask, free to answer, and free to start a new conversation. The Web site acts as a neutral space to support customers, exchange ideas, and get feedback about their products and services. The simple process involves finding a company or a product in question and typing in a question and sharing how you feel. Then a user will receive an e-mail notification when new activity occurs. At that point others can join in and say "me too." And finally, posting users will get answers from the company and the

Getsatisfaction community. In fact, Getsatisfaction has a widget you can incorporate into your company Web site to solicit feedback.

Similar to GetSatisfaction, SuggestionBox.com connects businesses with customers to build community and thereby build better relationships. The site works on the notion that a company should first listen to the customers to capture their ideas and suggestions and to show them that the company cares about them.

The site then leads the company to the second stage, which involves understanding the wants and needs of the customer as a way to learn what truly motivates them. In the third stage, the company responds to the customer's question, starting a conversation, literally, to dig deeper into what's underneath or prompting the question— the customer's wants and needs.

Lastly, SuggestionBox.com allows companies to connect with your customer and build a better long-term relationship. This can allow the company to improve on the things that matter to the customers, building customer loyalty as a result. After setting up a suggestion box, a company can then integrate it into their Web site for quick and easy reference. As a Suggestion Box.com user, the company will be provided with features to assist in managing, collaborating, and promoting the suggestion box to customers.

Blogpulse.com tracks conversations people are having about your company on the Web. Many companies now realize that this form of feedback is more insightful and honest than paid focus groups.

Which tools should your company use?

Lauren Freedman, president of the e-tailing group, states, "Community for many means ratings and reviews, while more progressive merchants test social networking depending on their customer base, inclination, and propensity to push the marketing envelope."

Manish Patel, of Where 2 Get It, sums it up: "Good customer service is listening to your customers, providing them the tool they need to make decisions, and understanding who the customer is today. Today the customer is in control, and they're looking to communicate with companies in many ways: by traditional phone, a Web site, mobile phone, and different types of social media. Listen to the way they want to communicate. Put yourself in their shoes and be open to any number of mediums."

Take action based on the feedback you get

Do you really want to know what your customers think? Can you conquer your fear of feedback? As Jack Nicholson said to Tom Cruise in the movie *A Few Good Men*, "You can't handle the truth." Many customers might not be willing to be honest with you, but some will tell you want they really think—and the more you demonstrate that you take their feedback seriously and actually change the way you are doing business based on what you learn, the more authentic feedback you will receive. And nothing is more critical to achieving *BAM!-good* customer service than inviting and receiving actionable feedback.

When you ask for an opinion, be ready to act on it or not. In 2007, the *Chicago Tribune* redesigned their newspaper. Readers were not pleased. Three months later, after thousands of comments, the *Tribune* published a review of the new format that stated what readers had said and what the *Tribune* was planning to do about it. This was impressive. Too many times, companies refuse to make changes in their products or services despite what people think. Taking action based on feedback sends a powerful message to customers that the company is listening and that it cares.

If you disagree with the feedback, then you still need to tell the customer why things will *not* change. When a company has a balanced two-way customer manifesto in place, customers understand that sometimes the answer to their requests will be *no*. This tells customers that you listened and considered their feedback, and there are good business reasons why the company will not change its process or procedures.

Depending on your level in the organization, you will have different goals for delivering customer service. Each person has an obligation to examine their role and responsibility for *BAM!-good* customer service, based on their level of authority and responsibility.

How to deliver for the CEO

The CEO determines the mission and the strategy that customer service plays in the business. How will the tactics of customer service support the overall mission of the company? The CEO has the responsibility to weave customer service into the company's DNA. If this does not happen at the CEO's level, then *BAM!-good* customer service cannot possibly successfully be implemented in the organization. As Craig Newmark, founder of Craigslist (who primarily works as a customer service rep), told us, following through with basic values like "treat people like you want to be treated," puts a company on the customer service track.

Mike Faith, CEO and president of Headsets.com, has "seven promises" that he makes to customers. A list of them is included with every order and they are prominently displayed on his Web site.[13] Mike tells us that the "seven promises" started as nine. "We thought, what are all the promises that might be important to customers? Nine was too many, so we compressed it into seven. They're promises which we think are hard for our competition to enact and valuable for customers who read them. It also gives our customers trust in us. We teach them to everyone in our four-week training program. And before anyone can go on the phones, they are required to know them completely. As part of our six-month testing process, they are also asked to remember and detail what they are and what they mean."

We have developed a list of questions that every CEO striving for *BAM!-good* customer service should ask.

1. **What is the mission of your company?** Be very careful about the context of the answer. Your mission, strictly speaking is to ensure the long-term sustainability of your business in return for meeting the expectations of the business's participants. But the CEO also needs to frame the mission in terms of the kind of relationship the company seeks with its customers and the value the company puts on helping customers feel satisfied.

2. **What does the customer mean to our mission?** Specifically, how will you use customer service to positively impact the financial bottom line—yours and theirs? What is the economic value proposition to your company for *BAM!-good* customer service? What are the important terms of your customer manifesto?

3. **Who is our customer?** As we have discussed, although there is no such thing as "the customer," the CEO needs to understand the target markets and clients, the problems those people have, and how the company will help solve those problems.

4. **How do I really feel about our customers? What is my attitude?** The actions that will produce *BAM!-good* customer service begin with the company's attitude. The company's attitude begins with the CEO. We believe that the CEO truly needs to love helping customers if customer service is to be part of the company's DNA. The CEO can't just pay lip service to it.

5. **What do I think we are doing right? What do I think we are doing wrong?** The CEO needs to examine at this very moment what the company is doing right and what the company is doing wrong. What effect is it having on the company's mission, and what will the impact be of making changes? How should changes be made, and what will their cost be?

6. **How am I personally going to stay in touch with customers?** When you are the CEO of even a small company, it is easy to lose touch with your customers as your organization grows and you become insulated. Many larger corporate CEOs do stunts where they carry bags at their hotels or run the fry machine at the restaurants. These are PR gimmicks and do not keep CEOs in touch with their customers. The CEO needs to have a systematic method for getting representative feedback from customers. Many CEOs schedule regular visits to their most important or frequent customers. On these visits, they ask penetrating questions and listen to what their customers say.

7. **What part of our customer manifesto do I own?** After the customer manifesto is implemented, what part does the CEO ensure stays effective? Every level of the organization needs to be responsible for a piece of it.

How to deliver for the manager

The manager's responsibility is to implement the strategy that the CEO has articulated through tactics. Questions the manager needs to answer are:

1. **What is the strategy the company will use to match our treatment of the customer to the importance of the customer to our company's mission?** We have stated this question in a very specific way. The manager needs to match their service of the customer with the level of importance the customer puts on the company. For example, our level of customer service has to be higher if we rescue stranded motorists rather than deliver dog food over the Internet.

2. **Who are our customers?** The CEO answers this question in the abstract. The manager needs to know the names and faces (if appropriate) of the most important customers in order to ensure appropriate actions. If you do not know who they are, find out now!

3. **What do I really feel about the customers?** Again, like the CEO, do managers in the *BAM!-good* customer service model love their customers? Sometimes interactions can be painful, but overall, do you enjoy them, knowing you make a difference in their lives?

4. **What characteristics/experiences are we going to look for in people we hire to be front-line customer service?** As we have discussed, people are key to the ability to deliver effective customer service. What characteristics do you need in your employees in order for them to be effective? For example:

- Friendly or serious

- Outgoing or reserved

- Generalist or detail oriented

5. **How are we going to train our people (front-line and not-so-front-line) in attitude and action/tactics so that our customers feel satisfied?** Forget common sense; what does your training program look like to ensure your people are effective? How do you monitor this? What follow-up training will you do on a consistent basis?

6. **What do I think we are doing right? What do I think we are doing wrong?** Like the CEO, the manager needs to examine at this very moment what the company is doing right and what the company is doing wrong. What effect is it having on the company's mission, and what will the impact be of making changes? How should changes be made and what will their cost be?

7. **How am I personally going to stay in touch with customers?** Again, it is easy to get insulated from customers and stand in back of your employees. Do you get on the line and take calls or help customers periodically? It is the only way to really see what the customer thinks.

8. **What part of our customer manifesto do I own?** You put together the manifesto with the CEO and now it has to be implemented and enforced. Which pieces do you own?

9. **How much decision-making power am I willing to delegate to front-line employees to empower them to deliver *BAM!-good* customer service?** What is the culture of our organization when it comes to empowering our employees?

How do we train them so we can enable them to make decisions for the customers when they need to?

10. **How will I put a process in place so that the front-line people can identify issues and suggest resolution?** We don't want to lose that intelligence. How do we capture feedback from the customer when it happens? This is best done by the front-line people. They need tools to be able to do this or the feedback will be lost.

How to deliver for the front-line employees

You are the person on the phone or over the counter with every customer. You are where results happen. You need to be clear in your own mind.

1. **How does the customer fit into my job?** Specifically, what are my responsibilities to the customer in my job? How do I interact with them and what effect do I have on delivering what they need?

2. **What is my priority for customers?** How does serving the customer fit into the priority of my everyday tasks? Clue: They may not always be number one!

3. **How do I really feel about customers?** Truly, even after a bad day, how do you feel about your customers? It is nearly impossible to stay in a front-line position if you do not truly love them.

4. **How do they feel about me?** Now it's their turn. How do you think they feel about you? How have they expressed their opinion about how they feel about you?

5. **What things about handling customers trip me up either in attitude or action?** Where do I not do my job as effectively as I could? Why? Is it the systems at the company, policies, or training?

6. **How much power do I have to decide what is right for the customer?** How much power have I been given to do what is needed for the customer? How much power do I need to achieve the objectives of my job and the company?

7. **What is the company doing right/wrong in dealing with customers?** You are on the front line and you are the one who knows. Your feedback is vital.

8. **How will I observe, capture, report, and suggest solutions to problems that keep repeating themselves?** This is a big part of your responsibility. It is your obligation to capture this feedback and report it. Do you have a way to do this, and is the company listening? Why or why not?

Customers are not one-size fits all

All this works great for most of your customers, but what about the customers that don't fit the norm—the customers who are your very best or the customers you love to hate? This is the topic of Chapter 7.

Chapter 7:
For Customers Who Color Outside the Lines: Delivering for the Best and Worst Customers

Every business has its favorite customers. These might be the clients who spend the most money with your company. They might be customers who are pleasant and easy to do business with. They might be the customers who signed up with you when you were just starting out. If you are in a service company, they might be the customers who have the most interesting problems or are willing to try the most inventive or innovative solution to gain an edge on their competitors. We all can name those customers who, for whatever reason, we think are so incredibly "valuable." We would do virtually anything to keep their business.

We also have other customers that we hate to love or love to hate. The polite label for them is "problem customers." We say it and roll our eyes. They are often the same customers who we knew on the first day of the relationship that "this customer is going to be a problem," but because of financial considerations at the time, we took them on anyway. You know the type: people who always find something to complain about or always want a little more discount than everyone else gets. These are the ones who cause us to cringe when we see them coming in the store or when we see their telephone number on caller ID.

Regardless of whether a customer is a favorite or dreaded, by now you know that we believe in going the extra mile to understand the uniqueness of each customer. We see that uniqueness as a basis for establishing the value of every customer relationship and as a basis for determining what *BAM!-good* customer service means for your business and the appropriate investment in customer service for your business.

When you know the financial value of a customer and how you really feel about that customer, you then have the information you need to rank and rate your customers and then evaluate which, if any, you want to treat differently.

And we do believe that it is good business to treat customers differently

Companies and their employees need this flexibility—not only to provide *BAM!-good* customer service, but for their own professional (and mental) health. Some clients we need to treat especially well. Some need to be fired for the good of your business and your employees. Be sensitive to the reality of both, and train your employees to figure out when and how to treat different customers differently.

Ways of treating customers are "special" in one industry and "meets minimum" or "business as usual" in others. For example, how long does it take your business to answer a request? What is your industry's standard? In the medical emergency business, response times are understandably compressed. While it is probably acceptable for your attorney to get back to you in twenty-four hours (unless, of course, you are in jail trying to make bail), this response time is never acceptable if you are in the auto-towing service or dispatching or driving ambulances.

Whether it is to reward or fire them, every business needs a system to understand their economically best and worst customers, as we have described in previous chapters. Review this quarterly. Information can be summarized from your accounting system customer by customer and by adding more qualitative metrics as discussed in Chapter 3. Once your company has this information, what types of things can the business do to treat the high-value customers?

Establish loyalty programs

The first loyalty or rebate program Barry can remember was S&H Green Stamps.[14] After shopping with our mothers in the 1960s, many of us came home with Green Stamps that merchants gave as a kind of bonus with purchases of groceries. We then pasted the Green Stamps into a book. The books of stamps could then be redeemed for all kinds of merchandise, from mixing bowls to bicycles. It almost seemed like magic—getting something for nothing. (We had little grasp of economics at eight and twelve years old.) Our mothers shopped only at the places that gave the Green Stamps. This was a loyalty program before frequent flyer miles.

Loyalty programs really took off when American Airlines started "American AAdvantage" in 1981[15], where flown miles could be redeemed for free trips and vacations. Car rental agencies were quick to jump on the bandwagon. These programs have expanded to credit cards, retail stores, car washes, grocery stores, gas stations, car rental agencies, and many other businesses. Frequent flyer airline miles have even become a second currency where a consumer can (not necessarily legally) buy and sell miles online.

One of the reasons loyalty programs have become ubiquitous is because the underlying principle makes sense to most of us. As we have repeatedly discussed, a seller/buyer transaction is exactly that—a transaction. The more money a customer spends with a business, the stronger the business relationship between the two. It seems logical that a company would want to treat its "best" customers specially and reward them in an appropriate fashion.

Barry has Executive Platinum status on American Airlines. Since he flies nearly one hundred flights a year, they treat him special. In fact, they should! He almost always sits in first class, and always gets on every sold-out flight on standby. The premise is that we have a choice of what airline to fly on, and given that choice, we get rewarded if we stick with one airline instead of always taking the most convenient time or the best price. Barry will pay 10 to 20 percent extra to fly American, and will even wait a few hours since he always sits in first class regardless of what he paid for his ticket. This is exactly why these programs have become so successful. In a world where United States domestic flying is really a commodity, this is the incentive to fly with one company. The United States government has almost given up trying to find a way to tax the benefits of the frequent flyer programs, and most companies now let their employees keep this perk. This is one of the few things in life that is almost free!

There are some very simple principles of a successful loyalty program:

1. **Determine a simple criteria and tiering for best customers.** This can be based on revenue or some other currency, such as visits. The important thing is to be sure that the way you keep score makes sense to all your customers—those who do a lot of business with you and those who don't. The popular gold, silver, and platinum levels are boring but effective. Everyone understands them.

2. **Prioritize the primary and secondary objectives of your program.** Let's be clear. We appreciate loyalty. Companies that treat customers with dignity and respect want to reward that loyalty—but the primary purpose of loyalty programs is to create velvet handcuffs to lock our customers in and have them come back even when they have a choice. This can be a good thing for the company and the customer, as Barry is reminded every time he has enough room to stretch his legs in an American Airlines first-class seat. The fact is that loyalty programs do change customer behavior without making customers feel boxed in or dissatisfied.

3. **Make it easy for customers to keep track of their points and to redeem them.** The best loyalty systems keep track of points electronically for their customers and report status periodically. As airline frequent flyers, we don't object that it may take a billing cycle to get credit for points earned by our MasterCard purchases. We are just grateful that we don't have to count the beans. The programs we don't like are the ones that force us to carry a card that the business punches or stamps to earn a free sandwich on every thirteenth order.

What is the likelihood that a customer will have that card twelve times? If Mary Jane kept every card in her wallet for programs like this, her purse would be heavier than it already is. Lettuce Entertain You Enterprises (LEYE) operates more than seventy restaurants across the United States. Their Frequent Diner Club helps the consumer earn points across all of these restaurants. Points can be redeemed for food, wine, and trips. There are three levels: blue, silver, and gold. What we like about this program is that they have one card (colored blue, silver, or gold) that consumers can carry that records the points earned and also collects the dollars redeemed. This makes it idiot-proof even for us.

4. **Establish a reward system that is flexible enough to remain consistent over time.** Nothing angers the very customers you are trying to keep more than changing the way they can cash in their rewards. Anticipate that if your program is successful, many people are going to accumulate points. If you don't want these points to accumulate indefinitely, set expiration dates in the beginning. It is always easier to announce that points will last longer than anticipated than it is to announce that they will expire earlier. A few years ago, airlines set expiration dates for miles retroactively, which caused a huge uproar among their loyal customers.

5. **Be absolutely circumspect about the way you use any marketing information you collect from these programs.** Obey the law regarding privacy and use of customer-supplied information, and then beyond those requirements to protect your customers' privacy. Publish your company policy on your Web site and display it in your place of business. Make it

easy for customers to opt out of marketing communications if they so choose.

Anticipate customer needs that are "regular" but "different" than those of most customers

Every business today should consider physical differences or limitations of any sort that their prospects or customers might have. From cut-curbs and ramps to accommodate wheelchairs to extra-length portions for seatbelts, to dairy- and nut-free products, every business needs to figure out what is right for them.

These considerations and respect for the dignity of all customers can become a differentiating factor for your business, and may even attract exceptional customers, assuming this is something that is desirable.

Another approach to this is separate lines. On Saturday mornings, and increasingly at other busy times, Post Offices have a special passport lines. The good thing about the line is that people who are there to mail packages and buy stamps are not slowed down by the forms and photos required for passports. The bad thing is that the passport line is always long—after 9 a.m., usually an hour or more.

Another good example of separate lines is the special lines at airport security. There are lines for the platinum airline customers, but there are also special lines for families with children. This makes things better all around—and is so sensible and considerate that it is kind of amazing that someone in the airline or security industry thought of it.

Businesses whose business is all about the unpleasant or hard times in life

There are businesses whose customers are going through difficult times. Often these are the businesses that have customers who feel the most satisfied. Take, for example, the undertaking and mortuary business. The customers of these companies are going through times of extreme sorrow. To be successful, funeral directors have to help people who are often going through some of the darkest and most bleak times of their lives feel satisfied.

Mary Jane grew up in a small town. Her family—from her great-grandparents on down—have depended on the Nunnelee Funeral Chapel to take care of things when someone dies. You know when you call them that every detail large and small will be handled professionally and unobtrusively. Mary Jane has always been amazed at how Tom Nunnelee, and his father Gene before him, could create such a safe and satisfied feeling for their customers. They listen. They understand what has to be done. They express clearly the decisions that have to be made. They respond to the family's priorities and do their best to satisfy those within the family's budget. They know how to make a few memorial flowers look lush, and they know how to make too many bouquets look less opulent. They know who to seat together and who to keep apart. They know more about the families in Mary Jane's hometown than possibly anyone, yet privacy is their utmost concern. The Nunnelee family could give lessons in customer service to those of us in other industries.

Also known for delivering great service are medical professionals and related businesses that serve oncology patients and their families. Talk about a situation where customers have a big problem to solve, yet how often do you hear cancer patients speak of the unfailing kindness of oncology doctors, nurses, and medical technicians? We can't think of an example of anyone we know who has had a bout of this terrible disease who didn't express gratitude and appreciation for the respect, consideration, and tenacity of their medical team, the American Cancer Society, the Y-ME organization, and others.

When special treatment has "unintended consequences" or what the heck were the marketing people thinking?

Sometimes treating customers specially affects other existing customers in unfortunate, unintended ways. This is when a company's efforts to treat customers specially or to offer unique incentives unintentionally fail. We are not talking about the fact that an Executive Platinum flyer can jump in front of an infrequent coach flyer. Most consumers understand that if you fly with an airline a lot, you will get VIP treatment and move ahead of the casual flyer.

Some companies, though, in order to attract new customers, give special incentives to new customers and call them "introductory offers." Why should a new customer receive an introductory price that is better than mine as an existing customer?

We know the marketing rationale—there is a cost (money or time) to customers who switch from whomever they are doing business with to a new supplier. People need enticement to make a move, but it does make loyal existing customers angry. Do you value a new customer more than an existing one? This again becomes a customer service policy of unintended consequences.

In January 2009, Banana Republic offered a special promotion to customers who were registered on their Internet site or who had purchased items in December. It was a card entitling the bearer to a 20 percent discount on their entire purchase, as long as they spent at least $100.

Mary Jane happened to be in Key West, FL, where there is a terrific Banana Republic store right on Duval Street. She had shopped there many times before. The sales associates are pleasant and helpful, and the store is well stocked. On this visit, she chose several items—the total was nearly $500. She took the clothing to the counter, and handed the sales associate her discount coupon and MasterCard. "This coupon doesn't go into effect until Monday," the associate said.

It was Sunday afternoon, about eighteen hours before the sale was to officially start. "I'm leaving in the morning about 9:30 a.m.," Mary Jane told her. "What time do you open?" "We don't open until ten," the associate said. "Could you charge my MasterCard the full amount today, then back it out tomorrow and charge me the lower price?" Mary Jane asked. "I'm sorry, we can't do that," the associate said. "There's no way to honor this coupon that goes into effect in less than twenty-four hours?" Mary Jane asked. "Sorry, no," the sales associate said, "but I can print out the item numbers and you can go to some other Banana Republic next week and use it."

Mary Jane left the store with only a $36 sale blouse. It made no sense for that store to allow a sale to walk out the door. Monday morning, when the Banana Republic that isn't too far from Mary Jane's house in Chicago opened, she called, but none of the items that had been in the Florida store were in stock in Chicago—it was warm weather on Duval Street and snowing on North Avenue. Nor were the items on the Internet. The bottom line: Mary Jane didn't spend almost $500 with Banana Republic. In fact, she hasn't spent anything with Banana Republic since that $36 blouse. It isn't that she's boycotting the store or anything. She likes their clothes and will go there again. The point is, what was Banana Republic trying to accomplish with that coupon? How do they train their people in customer service? What did they do right?

In the Duval Street store, the assistant was very helpful with sizes, colors, and choosing several separates that coordinated well together and that Mary Jane really liked. The sales associate took the initiative to print out the item numbers so that Mary Jane could ask for them when she returned to Chicago without having to try them on.

What could have turned this into the perfect customer service experience?

- Doing what Mary Jane asked: Charge her MasterCard for the full amount on Sunday, and credit it out on Monday and recharge it the full amount less 20 percent, honoring the coupon.

- Calling the Chicago store on the spot to see if they carried the merchandise, or offering to charge the merchandise the following day and ship it. Mary Jane wouldn't have expected the store to ship for free, but that would have been a really nice touch.

- Having some recognition that stores that are in travel destinations and resort locations may likely serve people who shop on Sunday and depart on Monday.

- Having an override provision for promotions and sales that would allow sales associates to honor the discount a day or two ahead of the published dates or a day or two after if in their judgment it would be the right thing to do.

Instead, what happened was that the Duval Street Banana Republic store lost a several-hundred-dollar sale. Mary Jane ended up being a dissatisfied customer, not because they were overtly rude, but because a program that some marketing person probably set up to entice people into the store at a slow time—January—in the middle of one of the worst recessions we've had in years, worked. Mary Jane went to the store, found clothes she liked, and was prepared to spend several hundred dollars, but because of some corporate policy (probably) she was denied the discount. She felt like something had been taken away from her and the store lost out. It makes absolutely no sense that Banana Republic would be willing to accept $80 for a $100 pair of jeans on Monday, but that they wouldn't honor that price eighteen hours earlier.

If you are going to offer promotions, imaging the experience your customer wants is an important exercise to go through and will typically yield the right answer. If you can, "mystery shop" and push the envelope at your own company—ask the store to honor a discount a day before or after the coupon period and see what type of service you receive.

A restaurant understands how to be flexible with a promotion

Mary Jane gives another example: My husband and I have a favorite neighborhood restaurant, RoseAngelis. It's a casual, welcoming place; we've been going there for more than fifteen years. The first week we moved into our neighborhood was the first week RoseAngelis opened, and we've had a special relationship with the owner ever since.

The food is delicious, the portions are substantial, and the prices are very fair. Often my husband and I share a salad and sometimes even an entrée and for sure a dessert.

Recently, the owner, who is a terrific marketer, began having a mid-week recession special of an appetizer to share, two Caesar salads, two entrées (anything from the menu or specials), and a dessert to share for $25 per person. The normal menu price could average around $35 per person, depending on the entrée a person chose. My husband and I were there with a guest. My husband wanted a soup appetizer and a salad; my friend and I wanted to share a salad and each have our own entrées. They didn't want dessert, but I did. We ordered the recession special for two and told our server, who was someone we didn't recognize, that we wanted to divide it up three ways. The server hesitated. "Is there a problem with doing that?" we asked. "They frown on that," she said. "Who is 'they'?" I asked her," knowing that the only "they" was the owner, who I was pretty sure would let us order any way we wanted because that is the kind of welcoming service he provides. We agreed that our server was probably new, and sure enough, a few minutes later she returned to the table, and said there was no problem splitting the recession special the way we had asked.

RoseAngelis is not a place where most people linger over their meals, although you are welcome to if you want. The portions are gigantic. They are very happy to send food home with you, and the restaurant is busy every evening.

Our experience on this one night illustrates several points that anyone in the restaurant business will likely understand.

1. Restaurants want repeat customers.
2. Food is perishable. If a person doesn't buy a dinner on one night, it is unlikely they will buy two dinners the next.

3. People shy away from restaurants that aren't busy. Jammed may or may not be good for business. Empty is always bad.
4. If a restaurant offers a special promotion, diners will find a way to max it out.

The whole point of the recession promotion is to bring diners into RoseAngelis. It's the principle of price elasticity to the max. Not only were my husband and I two regulars, we had a guest who had never been to the restaurant before. She ended up loving her meal and will certainly return and tell others about her experience.

At the conclusion of the meal, the owner sent a second dessert. The only flaw in this whole setup was that our server didn't automatically say yes, when we asked to split portions of their meals. Maybe she was new. Maybe she hadn't been asked that before. Maybe she made the decision she didn't think it was right—or maybe that's how they would have told her to answer at the last place she worked. It ended up being more than okay—the food was great, the extra dessert was thoughtful, the tab for three people was more than reasonable, and our guest had a great time, but all that didn't erase the small tickle that we felt when the server initially said no. My husband and I left with something slightly less than the perfectly satisfied and happy feeling we usually have when we take guests there.

Has this experienced dampened our long-standing enthusiasm for RoseAngelis? Absolutely not. My husband and I love RoseAngelis and its owners and employees. It is our first choice for dinner. The food and service are wonderful. We've been going there for almost twenty years and we expect to have dinner there for twenty more. We recommend it all the time.

The point of this story is how such a tiny sliver of a customer's total experience has the potential to affect the big feeling that the customer has for the company. Imagine what happens when an employee says "they don't do that" (meaning the company) to a customer who is neutral already, or who hasn't had a long record of excellent experience with the company. That customer is likely to go away and not return.

Firing a customer: Getting rid of those you, well, just love to hate

We all have those customers we hate to love or love to hate. We all have those customers we wish we could just fire. Can we? The answer is yes and no. Deborah House, CEO of The Adare Group, tells us, "I'm a firm believer in firing high-maintenance customers—unless they're willing to pay top dollar. If they call and scream at me on the phone, their fee just went up by 50 percent."

The first step is to put your emotions aside and understand the true economic value of the customer to your business. Only when you do, can you decide if your business can afford to fire this customer. You may be surprised after this evaluation that the customer who is problematic for your company really contributes very little to the bottom line. Even if their revenue is good, the extra expense—often not tracked—that it takes to accommodate them makes the overall value far less than it seems on the surface.

When this is the case, it is a fairly easy decision to show that customer the door. You may even take pleasure in it. However, if the problem customer has high value to your business, in spite of what it costs to take care of them, figure out one of two things: How to minimize the negative impact their behavior has on your employees, or how to replace the problem customer's revenue and other value before you fire them.

The first step is always to evaluate how you might continue to serve the customer while minimizing the extra resources they consume and the negative impact they may have on your team. One way to do this is to build a special team that handles "special" customers. When you set up a group like this, you must recognize that by definition the customers those employees serve require more time, create more frustration, and are by definition much more difficult to satisfy. This means that your "special needs" team must be individuals with extra patience, good judgment, authority beyond their job titles, and a sense of humor. This group still needs to set boundaries with these customers so that at every quarterly analysis, they are still profitable and don't require so much service that they fall into the "terminate" category.

You need to set up a special way of measuring their performance. Whatever that is, the way your company measures customer service output does not apply to this group. They are going to be less efficient. They are going to ask for things that you wouldn't or couldn't provide to all customers. These employees, compared to others that service customers, may feel like something of a pain, just as the customers they are handling do. Remember that you have decided that these are customers you want to keep. This is the cost of keeping them.

In our current careers as independent consultants, we have had high-economic-value customers that we needed to fire from our business. Our criteria for considering firing a customer—something we don't take lightly—are:

1. We are no longer helping them—either because they needed skills we don't have or we have taken them as far as they are able to go.

2. The customer is disregarding our advice. It makes no sense for them to pay for something they can't use.

3. The customer's core business is not going to work, and they are unwilling to consider a different approach.

4. The customer is not willing or able to pay a price that we can live with to make a profit.

5. The customer has asked us to do something illegal or unethical.

6. The customer has behaved inappropriately toward us or one of our employees.

When we reach the stage where we seriously question whether the relationship between our business and a certain customer should continue, these are the steps that work:

1. If the customer has behaved unethically, inappropriately, or illegally, seek the advice and counsel of your attorney and human resources departments to decide on an appropriate plan.

2. Revisit the economic value of the customer as a flinty-eyed accountant would, or have an outside unbiased resource do this.

3. If you wish to keep the customer, it is time to have a face-to-face discussion with them and set new boundaries that can work within the context of your company.

4. If the customer is not one that you would want to keep for economic reasons, there is no need to go further. Create a plan to terminate the relationship.

5. Before making this move, recommit to yourself and your employees that, in the long run, the business will be better off without this particular customer. This allows everyone to get over whatever emotion is there and move on.

6. Do not engage in or permit any personal discussion about the former customers. Do discuss what the business can learn from the experience.

7. Identify a series of prospects that can replace the problem customer. Refocus energy and resources toward marketing and selling to them.

8. Begin to phase the "fired" customer out of your business when you get these additional clients.

9. Show the problem clients other options for their needs (competitive alternatives), telling them that you are no longer the best to serve their needs.

10. Set an internal date at which you will no longer be doing business with the problem customer.

In following these steps, do not let your emotions drive the process. It is important not to let your emotions drive anything rash that would harm your business in the short or long term. Disengaging from a customer who represents substantial economic value to your business requires as much planning and finesse as it took to develop this customer in the first place.

Chapter 8:
Take Action:
What Do I Do Now?

In the end, why deliver good customer service? Susan Landa of The Fossil Cartel sums it up: "Because it helps make sales and helps make the bottom line. It's also good for morale. Being pleasant, friendly, and gracious makes it a better workplace."

Step 1: *BAM!* your own company and bust your own myths now

We all need to *BAM!* Every company first needs to examine how customer service myths are getting in the way of its business goals and undercutting effective customer service plans. What do we believe that just isn't true? What is not working in our companies? Businesses need to ask themselves the following questions. (Some of the ways you can answer these questions have, of course, been described in this book.)

1. Have you replaced the myth of "the customer" with the recognition that there is no one customer; that—as inconvenient as it may be for a business that wants to deal in economies of scale—every customer is unique with individual desires, needs, and feelings that can change in a blink?

2. Are you running your company with the attitude that customers are always right? Do you ask employees to make so many concessions that *they* feel walked over? Have you achieved trusting relationships with customers so that there can be a balanced give-and-take?

3. Is the company's true belief (as shown by its action and attitude) that the customer is always wrong? Do you talk down to or make fun of any customers when they aren't around? Whether they overhear you or not, this will show in your front-line employees' attitudes.

4. Do you concentrate your resources on producing the best-quality products, believing that quality is a substitute for providing after-sale customer service? How has this worked out for your company?

5. Do you consistently provide specific and customized customer service training to your front-line employees, or do you rely too heavily on human resources' assurances that you are hiring the best quality and most experienced people available? Do you expect your employees to learn in the line of fire or to take what they've learned from their previous experience?

6. In your company, is customer service treated as a professional responsibility or as an afterthought? Is it respected and seen as an important trait?

7. Do you secretly wish your business did not have to deal with customers? Be honest and truthful. What role do customers play in your organization?

8. Do you limit your pursuit of new customers, believing that if you just service your current customers in an outstanding way that your business will prosper?

9. Do you service customers only out of the fear that if you don't, they will say bad things about your business to other people?

10. Have you given up and accepted the fact that some customers will just be unhappy no matter what you do? Do you keep customers long after they should be fired?

11. Do you believe that your customers should be patient or that some of their expectations are unreasonable? Do their needs strike you as needy? Did you have any part in setting these unreasonable expectations?

12. Does your company just focus on low price as its sole criteria for customers to buy your products over the competitions?

13. Do you hire people who bring with them an established customer base or the kind of people that customers already like?

14. How do you get feedback from your customers about the quality of service you provide? Do you base your customer service evaluations and decisions on comment cards that customers fill out without questioning their validity?

15. Do you believe the best way to a happy customer is to under-promise and over-deliver? If you do believe this, how do you decide what to promise vis a vis what you are able or intend to deliver?

16. Do you believe that one customer service policy fits all of your customers?

17. Get all the grumbles out! Who or what are you complaining about now?

Step 2: Define customer service for your company as you want it to be

1. *BAM!-good* customer service is defined by those **actions and attitudes** that a business takes and holds that help a customer *feel* more satisfied. Before your company can create *BAM!-good* customer service, you need a handle on how customer service is today.

2. List your company's attitudes toward the customer as individuals. Do you like the people who do business with you? How do your employees feel about your customers? Just how badly do you want your customers to feel satisfied?

3. What deliberate actions do you take with the specific intention of making your customers *feel* more satisfied? How are you building a dependable link between your company and your customers to produce the feelings you want your customers to have?

4. How do you know that you and your employees are listening—really listening—to your customers? Do you change how you are doing business based on what you hear from them?

5. Where do you think your company could be wasting money or other resources on actions that were intended to improve customer service but aren't?

6. Do you have a regular process for learning from front-line employees the things that make customers unhappy or dissatisfied?

7. List the ways your company treats customers with dignity and respect.

8. Describe your view of the perfect customer experience with your business. Ask your employees to describe the perfect customer experience with your business. Call up some customers and ask them to describe their view of the perfect customer experience with your business. Ask questions. Ask a lot of them. Ask them often in many different ways to get a true picture.

9. List the ways that your company treats customers that you wouldn't want to be treated yourself. If you don't think there are any, invite some of your front-line employees to enlighten you.

10. What would be the criteria and conditions under which you would fire a customer? Make a list of the customers you should fire. Create a time line to get this accomplished.

Step 3: Determine the economic value of your customers

Every company needs to identify the specific economic value that customer service has to their business. Throw out the pride, ethics, and altruism argument as the prime motivator for your customer service policies. Only through established economic value and benefits will you—and therefore the managers and other employees in your organization—become committed to *BAM!-good* customer service enough to follow through on it.

Select the factors that are most valuable to your organization and then work out the value of each customer.

1. **Revenue:** How much money does this customer pay you monthly/quarterly/annually?

2. **Timing:** What is the customer's accounts receivable history? Do they pay on time or do you have to dun? Do they pay with cash, by check, or by credit card?

3. **Referrals:** Have they ever referred anyone to you? Did that referral do business with you? Did that referral refer someone else? How much revenue did those referrals produce? Were they the types of customers you want?

4. **Opportunity for increased revenue from this customer:** Could this client purchase additional products or services from you? What is the potential dollar value of these sales?

5. **Feedback they give you:** Does this customer give you feedback that you can use to improve your business—verbally, on surveys, on comment cards, or on the Web?

6. **Stickiness:** How easy or likely would it be for this customer to leave you and do business with someone else? Have they ever left and returned? Have they decreased (or increased) their business with you in the last twelve months?

7. **Brand power:** Do you have a competitive edge with this customer?

8. **Unhappy customer:** Has this customer ever been unhappy with you? Have they ever complained? Have any of your employees ever complained about them?

The appropriate weighting of these factors depends on the kind of business you are in, the overall health of your business, and your growth and profit objectives. Considering these, develop a scoring formula following the example in Chapter 3.

Step 4: Tackle the *BAM!* Blockers

Identify the inhibitors and roadblocks within your own company that are keeping your commitment to excellent customer service from translating into action.

1. What beliefs do you and the employees in your company hold that are blocking *BAM!-good* customer service? Do you think it costs too much? That customers don't really care? That *BAM!-good* customer service is an unachievable goal? Dig deep and write down those beliefs. Only when you identify them can you start to get rid of them.

2. What processes and systems—automated or otherwise—don't work inside your company? If you think everything is working fine, you are wrong. Talk to the employees who are using them. You'll be amazed at how creative front-line people are. Often improvements are simple to make and don't cost all that much.

3. Do you set yourself, your company, and your employees up for failure by establishing unreasonable or unachievable customer service goals? Climbing a mountain is admirable; promising to fly without wings or a plane is stupid.

4. Talk to employees to uncover the excuses that exist in your company for *not* providing *BAM!-good* customer service. Write down their excuses and yours—and develop a plan to overcome them.

5. Has your company's ability to deliver customer service changed? Are resources tighter (or more plentiful)? Have you lost key customer service personnel—either in management or in floor leadership? Has your competition become better or less of a threat?

6. Identify where company talk doesn't match company walk. What are you saying about customer service that is at odds with the quality of service you want to deliver or the company's stated goals?

7. What is your plan to deal with the unavoidable challenges of providing *BAM!-good* customer service? How are you going to keep customers satisfied when they have to wait on the phone, in line, or for a period of time while you take the steps to fix their problem—to order parts, schedule the best technician, send replacement merchandise, etc? How do you handle it when you can't solve customers' problems at all?

Finally, listen to the people who are doing the job. Tracey Welsh from Red Mountain Spa says, "While I may know the best practices or have good experiences, for your facility to have an individual flavor and stand out and be unique, the employees are going to tell you what the guests want. If you are dictating to the employees what the guests want, they aren't going to buy into it. If the employees are allowed to have their own passions and allowed to develop that level of customer service, you will get it."

Step 5: Write your own manifesto

Every organization needs a manifesto. You can modify the one in the appendix of this book or customize a unique manifesto of your own by answering the following questions:

1. What have we promised we will deliver?

2. How is our company committed to resolving the customers' issues in a reasonable manner? What are our practices and policies on refunds?

3. When things go wrong, is our company easy to contact in an economically feasible manner? Do we provide our customers an easy-to-find-and-follow way to talk with a live person? If not, why not? How could we supply this information?

4. How does our organization admit to mistakes? Do mistakes cause our company to change the way we do things to improve, or do we justify our behavior and stay stuck? Do we wait for customers to tell the company that we've made a mistake, or are we proactive? When we know there's been a mistake, do we alert customers before they bring it up? How do we make it right for everyone before they complain, or do we wait for customers to call and then react?

5. How do we empower our employees to solve customers' issues when and where they occur without having to wait for or seek out a manager? If a customer asks to speak to a manager, is that manager readily available? How do we structure an escalation procedure—that we hope we never have to use?

6. In what ways would our customers say that our company is already easy to do business with?

7. Is there an easy way for a customer to end their business relationships with you if they desire?

8. Do we charge separate nuisance fees or surcharges? How can we get rid of them, even if it means raising our prices?

9. When our company changes terms, products, prices, or practices, do we have a consistent and reliable way to tell customers in advance? How can we improve this communication?

10. Do we ever give or sell any information about our customers without asking their permission in advance?

11. In what ways do we invite our customers to provide their feedback? How do they know we are listening? What do we do with their feedback? Does it influence or change our behavior? How do we respond to them?

Step 6: Decide the tools for measuring and how you are going to deliver

There are so many tools available to measure customer service. Decide which internal and external tools you will use to measure what you need based on the value you have identified by asking the following questions.

1. What social media resources will you track on the Web to see what customers are saying about you? Who will be responsible for this?

2. How can you take advantage of Facebook, LinkedIn, MySpace, Twitter, Yelp, or other similar tools?

3. How can you use technology to enhance the customization and personalization with the customer so they feel like they are being treated as individuals and that they stand out to your company as the individuals they are?

4. What survey questions are appropriate for your business, and how should a survey be administered? When should you ask for feedback? Are you willing to take action based on the results?

5. Before you tackle social media tools, be sure your company has all the "usual" aspects of customer service in place and working smoothly—employee training, call center processes and scripts, product quality, and problem-resolution processes.

6. Who will be tracking comments customers are making about you on the Web? How can you influence these fairly and positively? What non-company sites—places your customers frequently visit to chat about their experiences with companies—do you need to track?

Step 7: Set up a plan to handle your atypical customers

Decide how you will handle the small percentage of customers who will always be dissatisfied, no matter what actions your company takes.

1. Do you continue to try to placate them for fear they will incite other customers to be dissatisfied, or do you take pre-emptive action, as Sprint did, and fire these customers?

2. How will you treat your most economically valuable customers? Will you implement a loyalty program? Refer to the guidelines in Chapter 7.

3. Be aware of the unintended consequences of loyalty programs or promotions and be ready to adjust when these occur.

4. How does your business accommodate customers with special needs? What is your intention?

Conclusion

BAM!-good customer service is achievable, but like everything else in business, it doesn't happen magically overnight. It is about eliminating the beliefs that get in our way. It is the result of attitude and action, embracing the belief that customers are individuals, examining how your company treats its customers, and honestly desiring to do things that will help them *feel* satisfied. It happens by ensuring that *BAM!-good* customer service is in the DNA of your company by being able to articulate to all employees the relationship between profit and customer service. It is understanding the customers you need to give preferential treatment to and the ones you need to fire. It is a commitment to a two-way company manifesto between you and your customers.

Remember Barry's button, and we can all develop the competitive sustainable advantage to build strong, profitable companies.

"Just give me good customer service and no one gets hurt."

Appendix:
Things You Want to Remember from This Book

Barry and Mary Jane are list-makers from the word *go*. Following are lists and lexicon from this book for your easy reference.

Customer Service Myths

Myth #1: "The customer" is a single thing or entity.

Myth #2: The customer is always right.

Myth #3: The customer is always wrong.

Myth #4: Customer service is about having high-quality products.

Myth #5: Customer service is just plain common sense.

Myth #6: The term "good customer service" means the same thing to everyone.

Myth #7: Ethics, pride, and altruism are all reasons for providing customer service.

Myth #8: If you learn how to "put up with customers," business will be great!

Myth #9: Taking care of the customers you have is more important than getting new customers.

Myth #10: Unhappy customers tell their stories to more people than happy customers do.

Myth # 11: Unhappy customers are a part of doing business. If you handle a customer complaint well, the offended customer will turn around and be an even more loyal customer.

Myth #12: Customers don't care about great service; they just want the lowest price possible.

Myth #13: Customers can't expect a company to fix all complaints overnight.

Myth #14: Forget about customer service; people buy from those they like.

Myth #15: Some people are naturally good at customer service.

Myth #16: Comment cards and customer surveys accurately measure customer service.

Myth #17: Customer service systems should focus on troubleshooting. If it isn't broken, don't fix it.

Myth #18: Companies achieve customer service by under-promising and over-delivering.

Myth # 19: You can satisfy all of the customers all of the time.

Myth #20: We left this last myth open so that you can supply a favorite myth of your own. What is the myth that guides your view of customer service? What is your belief and what is the reality?

The *BAM!-good* Customer Manifesto

1. We will deliver on what we promised.

2. If you are dissatisfied with our product or service, we will listen attentively to all your concerns.

3. When things go wrong, we will be easy to reach in an economically feasible manner.

4. We will resolve your issues in a reasonable manner and in a reasonable time frame, or give you a refund or compensate you in a manner that leaves you as satisfied as possible.

5. We will admit when we made a mistake.

6. We will empower our employees to solve your issue at the point it occurs.

7. We will not force you to buy something you do not want.

8. We will make it easy to end our business relationship.

9. We will not charge separate nuisance fees or surcharges.

10. We will treat you with respect and dignity at all times.

11. When we decide to change something in our agreement (raise or lower our prices, alter our hours, drop or add a service or product), we will tell you in advance in a very public way.

12. We will never, ever, ever give or sell any information about you without your permission.

13. We will not fill your e-mail or your mailbox with marketing material you don't want to see. We will make it easy for you to opt in or out of information that we send.

14. We will offer you several convenient ways to provide feedback on our products and services.

15. In every situation, we will ask you what it would take to make you *feel* satisfied.

BAM!-good Customer Value Calculation

Each of your customers will have a weighted score of 1 to 22.

<u>Revenue</u>: What is the customer's rank in terms of revenue?

- Bottom 25% - add **1 point**
- Bottom 50% - add **2 points**
- Top 50% - add **3 points**
- Top 25% - add **4 points**

<u>Timing (add **2 points**)</u>: What is this client's accounts receivable history? Do they pay on time? In cash/by check/by credit card?

<u>Referrals (add **4 points**)</u>: Have they ever referred any new prospects to you? Did that person do business with you? Did that person refer someone else?

<u>Additional products they buy (add **3 points**)</u>: Does this client purchase additional products or services from you? Could they in the future? What would be the dollar value of these sales?

<u>Feedback they give you (add **1 point**)</u>: Does this client tell you how they feel about doing business with you before they are unhappy enough to complain—verbally, on surveys, on comment cards, on the Web?

<u>Stickiness (add **2 points**)</u>: Have they been your customer for more than two years?

<u>Brand power (add **4 points**)</u>: Do you have a competitive edge with this customer?

<u>Unhappy customer (subtract **2 points**)</u>: Has this customer ever been unhappy with you? Have they ever complained? Have any of your employees ever complained about them?

BAM! Blockers

Beliefs, lamentations, and excuses block the delivery of good customer service. We challenge you to *BAM!* these *BAM!* **Blockers** from your company and your life.

1. Our company's economic models works only if front-line customer positions pay minimum wage.

2. The computer or manual support system I have stinks.

3. Customers are fundamentally unreasonable people who set out to prey on business owners, nicking away at profitability by asking for more than they are willing to pay for.

4. We believe in setting high goals and standards for our company, and higher expectations for our customers, whether we can deliver on those goals and expectations or not.

5. There is nothing we can do in customer service since our products in the marketplace are so far from perfect.

6. The business believes it is delivering customer service, when, from the customer perspective, clients are tolerating things.

7. Just because the customers aren't mad doesn't mean you are delivering good customer service.

8. What was customer service yesterday may not be seen as customer service today.

9. Conditions have changed and the company cannot deliver the same level of customer service as before.

10. The basic prerequisites for customer service are missing. Stop using that cell phone!

11. The company leadership is saying one thing about customer service, but acting a different way.

12. Employees don't like their jobs. They kick the cat, taking their frustration out on the customers.

13. The company doesn't train employees with the specifics of satisfying customers.

14. Customer service is just plain common sense.

15. The company has set a price point that doesn't leave enough margin to provide the level of service and/or quality that customers want.

16. It's inevitable that every business will keep customers waiting.

17. Customers want a human relationship, and not every business can provide that.

18. All businesses must use voice mail in order to keep expenses down.

19. Well-trained and well-intended employees will not make mistakes that cause problems for customers.

20. Employees may not be able to efficiently and cost-effectively address customer problems without degrading service in other areas.

21. Employees may take the time to find out what the customers really think and feel.

22. Employees may not figure out the right balance of authority and employee empowerment.

Survey Responses from
Self-Service Survey in Chapter 2

Customer comments often provide the most insight to their feelings of satisfaction or dissatisfaction. Here's what they told us about self-service kiosk experiences in their own words.

What responders liked most about self-service isn't surprising.

- "It saves time. Speed."

- "I am in control and feel more independence."

- "Less lines."

- "What I like the best is not having to deal with the idiot they hired to help me, which is regularly a problem with both airlines and grocery stores."

What people liked the least were also things we expected:

- "Vague instructions or when the machines break down"

- "When there is a problem and there is no one to help"

- "Exceptions not handled well"

Some survey responders thought of the machines as people:

- "[I don't like] when the machine thinks it's smarter than me."

- "Supermarket checkout is evil—you have to put items in a certain place or it freezes."

- "The annoying and repetitive voice at grocery stores... there should be a 'beginner' machine, and an 'expert' machine for those who don't want to hear the annoying voice."

Some missed the personal experience and the human contact:

- "The machines can't give you the extras—like an aisle seat."

- "[There's] no chance to say hello or ask questions."

Others did not blame the machine but other people in line:

- "The worst part is the slow people in front of me."

We did not expect these answers:

- "I feel nervous about mistakenly forgetting to ring something through properly and then getting confronted about 'stealing.' It's never happened, but it does make me avoid the self-serve often."

- "It bothers me that people have lost their jobs due to these machines, and society becomes more impersonal."

Some respondents wanted to be paid for their trouble:

- "I should be paying less to check myself out in a grocery store—there's work—identifying the veggies, etc. There should be a discount...or a benefit."

One respondent just threw up his hands in frustration:

- "If something goes wrong, you are back in another line again."

And one rant:

- "I resent being herded cattle-fashion through self-service lanes simply because the company is too cheap to staff 'regular' lanes sufficiently. I'm happy to pay premium prices for goods and services, if I feel as though I'm getting service. If I feel as a customer I'm being designed out of the process, I get very annoyed. They're not quicker 'cos you always get some lame-brain in front of you who cannot work the scanner; invariably one or more kiosks is 'down,' and as a result, the queues are just as long, so where's the value-add for me, the customer? Automated voice systems for PBX are in the same category—designed to put a layer between me as a customer and the business to whom I'm giving my hard-fought-for attention. Why do they do that? Sorry, I'll get off my soapbox now."

BAM!-Good Definitions from this Book

With so many business books out there, words can get confusing. Here are our definitions of words used in this book. We are not saying we are right; this is just what the words mean to us.

Action: What you need to do to create the perfect customer service experience from the customer's point of view. The opposite of *wait*.

Altruism: Believing that a company or individual should give good customer service because it is the charitable thing to do. This is not only wrong, but is unsustainable for a profitable business.

Attitude: Making decisions with the deliberate intent of helping a prospect or customer feel more satisfied.

BAM: Acronym for **Bust a Myth**. See **Myth**.

BAM!-good **Customer Service:** The attitudes and actions that a business takes to help a customer feel more satisfied.

Belief: What people think and accept as true. May not correlate with facts. Have great sticking power, even when they are wrong.

Boss: As in, "the boss." Person employees should not have to talk to make the customer feel satisfied.

Brand Power: If you are a small company that serves a large brand, you can use that customer's brand recognition to attract more customers to you. Customers love references from brand companies they recognize.

Chat: Talking through typing in real time to another person on the Web or your phone. This is what your teenage children spend most of their time doing.

Common Sense: There is no such thing in customer service. See **Training**.

Competitors: Individuals and companies who want our customers. If we are not providing *BAM!-good* customer service, they can and will take our customers.

Complain: What a customer does when they are unhappy. They complain to themselves, to friends, on the Web, and even sometimes to you.

Customer Service: Ah, you are not going to get away so easy. It is whatever the customer feels it is. Read the book we wrote!

Customer: There is no such thing as "the customer"; therefore, there are too many definitions to list them all here.

Customer-less: Either someone who is out of business or a business in the state of pure nirvana. You pick! See **Belief**.

Customization: See **Personalization**.

Dignity: As in treat people with. See **Respect**.

Disney: A place where most customers are always happy. This takes a lot of employee training.

Empowerment: Training employees to make decisions on their own to help a customer without talking to "the boss."

Ethics: Everyone needs them, but we don't offer good customer service because it is the right thing to do.

Feedback: Giving the customer the opportunity to tell you what they think at many different stages of interaction, and the opportunity to do it in many different ways depending on what is convenient and appropriate for them. Something smart companies listen to and take to heart. Associated with the Three Times Rule—if you hear something about your business three times, whether you like it or not, pay serious attention. It is probably true.

Forever: Relative time the customer feels they need to wait. See **Wait Time**.

Happy: An impossible dream that is sometimes worth the pursuit. No business strategy in the world can make all customers happy. See **Satisfied**.

High Quality: The belief that high-quality products solve all the problems of customer service; that with quality products, customer service is simple, even automatic. Nonsense!

Humans: Who every customer wants to talk to when they call your company.

Kick the Cat: What employees do when they take their frustrations out on the customer. Blowing a situation out of proportion. The kiss of death for a company.

Manifesto: Your company's public declaration of its commitment to customer service.

Measurement: The methods your business chooses to decide the value of each customer and overall customer service in your business.

Mistake: The hardest thing for the company (or the customer) to admit.

Monopolies: Companies that never have to give good customer service because the consumer has no (or very limited) alternative but to buy their service. The heavy-handed way some companies (that aren't monopolies) treat their customers.

My Manager: The person the customer is seemingly always getting passed to or who always gets blamed by the employee if something goes wrong. The catcher in "passing the buck."

Myth: Something you believe that really is not true; for example: You can satisfy all the customers all the time.

Overpromise: Making a commitment to a customer or to all customers that the company is not economically able to keep.

Patience: What businesses think customers ought to have. What customers think they have a lot of.

Peer Reviews: Online references written by customers on the level of quality or service in your company. Sometimes called *an open reputation system.*

Permission Marketing: The company's commitment never to give out the contact or any other information of any customer... and you better not.

Personalization: Company use of technology to tailor their marketing, products, and services to the preferences and desires of that one customer. Also called *customization.*

Pest: A customer the company may need to fire to be more profitable.

Pride: What management thinks is the key ingredient in providing good customer service. Not teachable or duplicable.

Promise: A solemn commitment to a customer that the company will honor and the customer will not forget.

Prospect: Someone who should be interested in your company's product or service. Almost as good as a customer.

Reality: The way the customers feel about your business.

Referrals: When a current customer recommends your products or company to someone who may be a potential customer for you. Referrals are highly desirable.

Refund: A word not in many companies' vocabulary. The easiest way to help a customer who feels dissatisfied.

Respect: The number-one goal of any employee in treating a customer. See **Dignity**.

Retention: What every company wants to do with all its profitable customers. See **Stickiness**.

Revenue Timing: When the customer buys from you. This may be more valuable, especially if they buy when the company needs revenue that month (counter cyclical).

Revenue: Sales; very important—but not as important as cash.

Roadblocks: Beliefs, systems, or people that get in the way of providing good customer service.

Satisfied: The kind of feelings that customers have that keep them coming back to you. The goal of excellent customer service is a customer who feels satisfied. This is different than feeling happy.

A satisfied customer will stay and many times be profitable. A good way to know how to satisfy a customer is to ask them this simple question: "What will it take to make you satisfied?"

Satisfying a Customer: Action on the customer's answer to the question above.

Self-Service: Tools such as kiosks and Web tools for customers to assist themselves. Not always linked to satisfaction, but increasingly linked to high expectations of a quick turnaround.

Stickiness: How long a customer stays with your business.

Streaming Video: Content displayed to the viewer in real time over the Internet.

Surcharges: Fees that are in addition to the price of the product and sales tax.

Survey: A mostly ineffective means of getting customer feedback, especially when the company bribes the customer to do it.

Suspect: Someone who should be interested in what you are selling.

Sustainable Competitive Advantage: The thing that will always beat your competitors, even if they have a better product or more money.

Training: What every employee needs to do a great job of customer service. This cannot be emphasized too much.

Under-deliver: Not meeting the service expectations you set with the customer. Slow poison, if not the kiss of death.

Unreasonable: What many customer service reps think every customer request is.

Value: The economic value you have to your customer. The economic value customer service has to your business.

Voice Mail Jail: Every customer's nightmare, especially if they do not get a call back. See **Forever**.

Wait Time: How long a customer has to wait to be helped on the phone or in line. For a customer, this seems like, well, see **Forever**.

Wild Goose Chase: When the customer never feels they can get their issue resolved since they are passed around the organization. See **Empowerment**.

BAM!-*good* Biographies—
people you heard from in this book

Carl Albrecht

In response to two snafus that prevented a customer from getting her toner, Carl bought the cartridges at retail and drove five hours through a blinding thunderstorm on a Friday night to make sure she got them in time. He's a little over the top on service, and he credits his ten years at Federal Express for making him that way. He's cheap on anything that adds no customer value, however. PointManagement offices are furnished in early IKEA. But this focus on a combination of obsessive service delivery and cost containment is what earned PointManagement recognition as Best IT Vendor at Hertz Corporation.

He is a savant with point-of-transaction computer hardware repair service, but don't ask him where he last put his keys. His favorite things (after his wife and two kids): Single malt scotch, the University of Wisconsin Fighting Badgers, Led Zeppelin, sailing, and platform tennis. He's available to discuss any of these topics with you at your convenience for as long as you wish. Carl's hero is Bethany Hamilton. You'll need to look her up if you ever need inspiration, because we're already over the 150 words allowed for this bio.

Russ Borrelli

Russ Borrelli is a founding partner of eSlide.com, a graphic design company specializing in presentations. For over twenty-five years, Russ has assisted executives with his combination of creativity and strong technical knowledge. His unique expertise lies in his ability to understand the client message and convert that into clear, concise, and effective graphics. Before forming eSlide, Russ worked with a myriad of clients as a freelance presentation designer. His knowledge has been leveraged for projects ranging from multi-billion-dollar mergers to intimate sales pitches.

Mike Faith

Mike Faith is a serial entrepreneur and is founder and CEO of Headsets.com, Inc. His company has grown from a $40,000 investment in 1998 to $31 million in sales last year. Mike credits "customer love" as the number-one reason. Mike's company has made three appearances on the Inc. 500 fastest-growing companies list, and was voted as one of the best places to work in the Bay Area for the last two years. Catalog Success awarded him Cataloger of the Year in 2005, and he recently won a Stevie Award for creating America's Best Customer Service Team. Mike is regularly quoted in business publications, including *Fortune Small Business*, *Business 2.0*, and *Inc*, and he contributes to the Kauffman Foundation articles on entrepreneurship. Mike lives in the East Bay of California, is married with two children, a recent convert to veganism, and loves playing polo on Segways.

His not-for-profit, www.reservedinners.com, holds dinners for celebrities with 100 percent of the proceeds going to charities.

Margie Heisler

Margie Heisler has many years of success in customer service and sales. Her commitment to excellence, along with an ability to inspire confidence and deliver client satisfaction, has won her accolades in several industries. Her background includes the development and management of special/private events and catering offices at many renowned restaurants in the Chicago metropolitan area, including the world famous Le Français. Margie also led the office of special events and public relations at Lake Forest Academy, a prestigious private college-prep high school. There she established and coordinated annual events and fundraisers that attracted participation from across the globe. Heisler's keys to success are understanding the needs of her clients, paying close attention to detail, and creating realistic action plans and processes to achieve even the most ambitious goals and objectives.

Deborah House

As founder of The Adare Group, Deborah works with CEOs to maximize profits. Since 1981, increasing profits by record amounts through the dissection and examination of external forces, rather than indiscriminate expense reduction, has been her sole focus. She has obtained tens of millions of dollars in financing for growing businesses, including McDonald's franchisees, with debt and equity. Her financial knowledge and business acumen allow her to quickly develop and implement practical solutions with results that show up on the bottom line.

She structured successful mergers and integration activities, and developed and implemented strategic plans to increase profitability— plans that included strategic segmentation of customers and asset portfolios and operational efficiencies. Deborah is a CPA who has a wealth of experience in executive positions at companies such as McDonald's Corporation, Amoco Corporation, GATX, and Fifth-Third Bank. Her outstanding business acumen and financial expertise, plus a firm commitment to achieving results, have made her an asset to every organization.

Scott Jordan

Scott Jordan is the Founder and Chief Executive Officer of SeV and SCOTTEVEST. Before founding SeV, Scott practiced real estate and corporate law. But the law bored Scott; he was always an entrepreneur at heart. He received his bachelor of science in business administration from Ohio State University (OSU), majoring in entrepreneurship. He started Images Calendar Line while at OSU, and then went into a family business. Scott's accomplishments with SeV have appeared in articles in *The Wall Street Journal* and *New York Times*, among many other magazines and newspapers, as well as several college textbooks. Scott has since been featured on many TV shows, including CNBC's *The Big Idea* with Donny Fine; Living Network's *Radical Sabbatical*, and Japan's hit show *The World's Most Successful People*.

Susan Landa

Susan Landa, owner of The Fossil Cartel, has business ownership in her blood. While she was growing up in the New York City area, her father owned a wholesale ice cream company and would put Susan to work with him on days off from school. After ice cream, her first career was designing, crafting, and selling beaded jewelry all over the United States. Susan's beadwork progressed into jewelry featuring a marriage of beads and gemstones. To share her passion for the gem and fossil kingdom, in 1989 she opened The Fossil Cartel, a gem and mineral store in downtown Portland, OR, and online at fossilcartel. com. In 1987 Susan opened Let It Bead, a full-service bead store. Today she is an entrepreneur who owns and operates two retail stores in Portland, while developing a third business.

Shelly Malkin

Shelley Malkin of Perl Mortgage has been working with customers for over twenty years. As a healthcare administrator, Shelley consulted with federally funded community health centers to improve their operations, and at two major academic medical centers in Chicago, where she helped doctors transition from residency to private practice, and helped them provide the best services to their patients.

When Shelley bought her first home with her husband, she became fascinated by the Chicago real estate market and launched her career helping customers with all aspects of financing their homes. She met her first customer by showing up uninvited at a realtor's open house on a holiday weekend, and has been building relationships ever since. Now a ten-year veteran in the mortgage industry, Shelley is still passionate about customer service.

Marshall Makstein

Marshall is the president of eSlide, a graphic design company that specializes in professional-quality presentations that communicate information quickly, accurately, and effectively. eSlide has hundreds of clients and works with top executives of some of the largest companies in the world.

Marshall co-founded this company seven years ago, because he believes a presentation can be one of the most important corporate communication tools available today. With over twenty years in the industry, he has seen the best and the worst of presenters. But most important, he has seen how a good presentation can have a tremendous impact on a company's future.

Manish Patel

Manish is CEO of Where 2 Get It, a premier provider of intelligent location-based marketing services geared toward channel development companies. Manish's client service and management philosophies have enabled the company to grow its customer base to more than 280 clients and 130 consumer brands that include Polaroid, La-Z-Boy, Mitsubishi, and Reebok.

JoAnne Pavin

JoAnne Pavin, owner of Soulutions to Health, has been helping people live more energetic lives through one-on-one consultations, group retreats, and healthy products for more than fourteen years. JoAnne specializes in stress management, offering education and services such as massage, yoga, exercise, and weight management throughout the Chicago area. Her success as a small business owner, entrepreneur, and health advocate has been built on the power of customer satisfaction and referrals.

After successfully failing at a product start-up in the early 2000s, she met Barry, whose business and mental mentoring saved her from the entrepreneurial junk yard, and propelled her to the next career phase—writing a book. Her mission to understand cultural health and healing has led her to many countries, including India, where she studied in affiliation with the International Academy of Ayurveda.

Debbie Rosas

Dedicated to lifelong self-healing and mastery, Debbie Rosas has been a pioneer and a leader in the body-mind fitness industry since 1976. Her extensive exploration of dance, martial arts, fine arts, music, therapy, and healing work inspired and developed into the creation of

Nia Technique, an internationally acclaimed program offered in gyms and fitness clubs, spas, wellness facilities, martial arts centers, dance and theater departments, college-accredited PE programs, drug and alcohol rehabilitation, sexual abuse centers, and cardiac-rehabilitation clinics worldwide. As part of the Nia Technique, Debbie's work includes the production of eleven DVD workouts and meditation tapes, and over fifty instructional DVDs.

Together with creative partner Carlos Rosas, Debbie has co-authored two books, *Non-Impact Aerobics* and *The Nia Technique*, as well as the "Holistic Fitness" section of the *AFAA Instructor Training Manual*. Today, Nia Technique, Inc. is a thriving training and education business, operating in more than thirty-seven countries with approximately 2,200 Nia teachers worldwide.

Terry St. Marie

Terry St. Marie is the senior vice president of operations of Bresnan Communications, a cable television operator in Montana, Wyoming, Colorado, and Utah. Since 2003, he has managed the field operations, call centers, and network operations center, a group that has achieved industry-leading benchmarks in numerous customer satisfaction and service metrics.

Terry joined the company in 1994 to supervise all operational activities of Bresnan's international ventures and strategic partnerships, which were eventually sold in 1999. From 1999 to 2003, he played a key role in new business development for the company.

Jennifer and Eric Warden

Jenny and Eric Warden are the owners of Mustang Elite Car Wash in Grapevine, TX, a destination car wash and gift boutique that specializes in consistently providing the highest quality in car care and maintenance in a welcoming and friendly atmosphere. Prior to becoming a business owner, Jenny was a national sales leader in employment outsourcing for the technology industry. Eric was in mergers and acquisitions in the waste management industry.

Mustang Elite specializes in offering loyalty programs with a personal touch that their customers like. Together, the Wardens are building an enterprise of car washes and lube centers while contributing to the economy, school spirit, and quality of life of the communities they serve. Mustang Elite customers say that the Wardens' focus on service is the difference-maker, and that Mustang's courteous and well-trained employees and the cool merchandise in the lobby boutique keep the car wash busy, even on cloudy days.

Tracey Welsh

What's not to love about a job in the red rocks of Southern Utah, where you are surrounded by vacationers and people trying to improve their health! As general manager at Red Mountain Resort & Spa, it's a dream come true. Tracey carried a bachelor's degree in radio/ TV communications management into a Midwestern golf resort over twenty years ago, which led her through the ranks and eventually on to the executive team. However, the warmth of the southwest, along with the mission of Red Mountain, convinced Tracey to relocate to join the Red Mountain Spa team in 2001 as director of operations, and she was promoted to general manager in 2006. While you are here, you can find her throughout the resort, as she enjoys welcoming guests and hearing about their Red Mountain adventures.

Notes

[1] Author interview, April 13, 2009.

[2] "Sprint to 1,000 Customers: You're Fired," MSN Money, July 9, 2007.

[3] Cornish, A. "Zappos Proves Shoes Do Sell Online." National Public Radio, July 14, 2007. http://www.npr.org/templates/story/story.php?storyId+11980729.

[4] We did not include gas stations because, except in Oregon and New Jersey, the driver typically does not have a choice but to pump their own gas.

[5] Godin, S. Marketing the Cow with a Cow. http://www.sethgodin.com/purple/chapter.html.

[6] Motivational poster sold on www.Despair.com.

[7] Author interview, March 16, 2009.

[8] Chafkin, M. "The Zappos Way of Managing." Inc. Magazine. http://www.inc.com/magazine/20090501/the-zappos-way-of-managing.html.

9   Chafkin, M. "The Zappos Way of Managing." Inc. Magazine. http://www.inc.com/magazine/20090501/the-zappos-way-of-managing.html.

10 www.netpromoter.com.

11 http://www2.motivequest.com/survey/Survey aspx?id=yA8Ah0bTJWc%3d.

12 Omidyar, P. "Founder's Note to the eBay Community." Feb. 26, 1996. http://pages.ebay.com/services/forum/feedback-foundersnote.html.

13 http://www.headsets.com/headsets/7promises/index.html.

Headsets.com 7 Promises

Satisfaction Guaranteed

Our 60-Day Unconditional Money Back Guarantee means that if for any reason (or no reason) you're not absolutely delighted with your purchase from Headsets.com, you may exchange for any other product you'd prefer to try, or you may return the products and receive a prompt and courteous refund, no questions asked.

Compatibility Guaranteed

Our headsets are compatible with 98% of phones; as specialists, we know what works. In the rare event that we supply a headset that is incompatible with your phone, you'll receive a refund and we'll send you a FREE return shipping label.

Fast Live Help

Your phone call will be answered by a live person, based in San Francisco, who is eager to help. It's our goal to answer all calls in 4 rings, but if we can't take your call right away we promise to call you back within two business hours. If you click on 'Instant Live Chat' at our website you'll receive a live response within 60 seconds.

Full Replacement

All products carry a one-year full replacement product warranty, and corded office telephone headsets and amplifiers carry a two-year full replacement product warranty. We'll replace any faulty product without hesitation, so you know that you'll never have to wait for a repair.

Free Lifetime Product Support

It should only take a few minutes to unpack your new headsets, connect them, and make your first call. You're welcome to make that first call to Headsets.com. We'll gladly help you to fine tune the volume controls so you speak and hear with crystal clarity. Our headset specialists are on call at 1-800-432-3738 Mon. - Fri. 6:00am - 4:30pm PST.

Management Accountability

We promise you efficient and friendly service at all times. If you're not satisfied, neither are we. Our managers are available to address any concerns.

[14] S&H Green Stamps (also called Green Shield Stamps) were a form of trading stamps popular in the United States between the 1930s and late 1980s. They formed a rewards program operated by the Sperry and Hutchinson company (S&H), founded in 1896 by Thomas Sperry and Shelly Hutchinson. During the 1960s, the rewards catalog printed by the company was the largest publication

in the United States, and the company issued three times as many stamps as the U.S. Postal Service. Customers would receive stamps at the checkout counter of supermarkets, department stores, and gas stations, among other retailers, which could be redeemed for products in the catalog. Source: Wikipedia.

[15] "History of Loyalty Programs." http://www.frequentflier.com/ffp-005.htm.

Index

A

Action 4, 19, 27, 28, 29, 31, 37, 53, 58, 90, 107, 118, 122, 123, 125, 129, 140, 145, 146, 167, 168, 173, 176, 177, 187, 192, 196
Admirals Club 42, 43, 62
Albrecht, Carl 44, 90
Alexander, Andy 4
Altruism 9, 52, 54, 55, 82, 132, 171, 179, 187
Amazon 2, 9, 10, 14, 87, 136, 137
American Airlines 39, 42, 43, 62, 152, 153
Apple 6, 7, 91
ARDIS 58, 59
AT&T 59, 84
Attitude 4, 19, 23, 26, 29, 31, 37, 58, 70, 78, 81, 102, 103, 118, 120, 126, 133, 143, 145, 146, 168, 177, 187

B

BAM! Blockers 75, 77, 173, 182
Banana Republic 157, 158, 159, 160
Belief 4, 5, 6, 7, 8, 9, 10, 11, 12, 13, 14, 15, 16, 17, 18, 19, 81, 168, 177, 180, 187, 188, 189
Blogpulse.com 139
Borrelli, Russ 27, 45, 194

Boss xiv, 187, 188
Brand Power 65, 66, 69, 172, 187

C

CEO 6, 31, 61, 77, 81, 89, 90, 125, 128, 134, 141, 142, 143, 144, 145, 163, 195, 199
Chat 28, 105, 135, 177, 187, 205
Chicago Transit Authority 40, 107
Chicago Tribune 140
Coca-Cola 63
Common Sense xix, 7, 8, 91, 145, 179, 183, 188
Competitors 33, 82, 83, 98, 149, 188, 192
Complain 12, 17, 39, 51, 65, 67, 98, 121, 122, 150, 175, 188
Costco 76, 93, 94
Craigslist 141
CTA 40, 41, 107
Customer Manifesto 101, 102, 116, 141, 142, 143, 145, 181
Customer Service Rep 9, 59, 141
Customer Value Calculation 65
Customization 87, 176, 188, 190

D

Disney 46, 47, 48, 93, 188

E

eBay 14, 136, 137, 204
Elliot, Christopher 74
empowerment 96, 183
Empowerment 188, 193
Ethics 9, 52, 179, 188

F

Facebook 11, 61, 114, 135, 176
Faith, Mike 141, 195
Feedback 6, 12, 17, 56, 57, 65, 66, 68, 86, 89, 113, 115, 121, 125, 126, 127, 129, 131, 132, 133, 135, 136, 137, 138, 139, 140, 141, 143, 146, 147, 169, 172, 176, 181, 188, 192, 204
Freedman, Lauren 28, 139

G

GetSatisfaction.com 138
Godin, Seth 11, 203
Great Recession 60

H

Hammacher Schlemmer 117
Heisler, Margie 94, 195, 196
High Quality 189
House, Deborah 6, 89, 95, 96, 163, 196

J

Japan 78, 79, 197
Jordan, Scott 38, 134, 135, 197

L

Landa. Susan 30, 32, 78, 79, 167, 197
Lexus 48, 85

M

Makstein, Marshall 19, 135, 198
Malkin, Shelly viii, 31, 40, 118, 198
McDonald's 6, 96, 102, 103, 196
Measurement 22, 189
Microsoft 63, 64, 83, 84, 85, 93, 119
Mistake 31, 32, 89, 106, 175, 181, 189
Motivequest 204
Myth 1, 2, 4, 5, 6, 7, 8, 9, 10, 11, 12, 13, 14, 15, 16, 17, 18, 26, 28, 29,
    31, 52, 61, 62, 69, 70, 75, 76, 80, 81, 83, 85, 90, 91, 105, 116, 168,
    179, 180, 187, 190

N

Net Promoter 129, 130
Newmark, Craig 141
Nordstrom 5
Nunnelee Funeral Chapel 156

O

Omni Hotels 44
Oriental Trading Company 106
Overpromise 190

P

Patel 31, 61, 125, 140, 199
Patience viii, 14, 41, 91, 105, 164, 190
Pavin, JoAnne 94, 199
Peer Reviews 190
Permission Marketing 190
Personalization 87, 176, 188, 190
Pest 123, 190
PETCO 16
Portland Paramount Hotel 87
Pride 9, 51, 52, 54, 82, 132, 171, 179, 190
Promise xiii, 101, 116, 117, 118, 119, 169, 191, 204, 205
Prospect 15, 19, 37, 38, 42, 48, 68, 70, 72, 130, 187, 191

R

Rabjohns, David 128, 134
Reality 4, 5, 6, 7, 8, 9, 10, 11, 12, 13, 14, 15, 16, 17, 18, 26, 28, 32, 150,
    180, 191
Referrals 56, 60, 65, 66, 67, 172, 191, 199
Refund 105, 106, 120, 123, 181, 191, 204
Respect 24, 25, 37, 38, 78, 82, 87, 113, 115, 134, 153, 155, 157, 171,
    181, 188, 191
Retention 63, 191
Revenue xiv, xvi, 49, 55, 56, 57, 58, 59, 60, 63, 64, 65, 66, 67, 81, 82, 84,
    112, 132, 153, 163, 172, 191
Revenue Timing 60, 191
Ritz, Césare 5
Roadblocks 74, 75, 99, 173, 191
Rosas, Debbie 39, 199, 200
RoseAngelis 160, 161, 162
Rosner, Bob xiv

S

Self Service 125, 184, 192

S H Green Stamps 151, 205
Smart Car 112
Southwest Airlines 6, 13, 76
Sprint Cellular 25
Starbucks 97
Stickiness 63, 65, 66, 69, 172, 191, 192
St. Marie, Terry 134, 200
Streaming Video 135, 192
SuggestionBox.com 139
Surcharges 111, 112, 113, 175, 181, 192
Survey 12, 36, 87, 94, 127, 128, 129, 131, 134, 176, 184, 192, 204
Suspect 192
Sustainable Competitive Advantage 192
Swine Flu 108

T

Tokyo 38
Training 8, 22, 78, 80, 81, 90, 91, 92, 104, 107, 120, 129, 142, 145, 146, 168, 176, 188, 192, 200
TSA xix, 88
Twitter 11, 61, 135, 176

U

Under-deliver 192

V

Value 50, 51, 53, 55, 56, 57, 58, 61, 64, 65, 66, 69, 70, 72, 81, 82, 95, 101, 105, 108, 114, 142, 150, 151, 157, 163, 164, 165, 166, 171, 172, 176, 186, 189, 193, 194
Verizon 59

W

Wait Time 9, 92, 189, 193
Wal-Mart 15, 78
Warden, Jennifer and Eric 48, 58, 60, 200
Washington Post 4
Welsh 89, 95, 97, 174, 201

Y

Yelp 11, 137, 138, 176

Z

Zappos 8, 33, 34, 77, 81, 203, 204